Generative AI and Libraries
Claiming Our Place in the Center of a Shared Future

Michael Hanegan and Chris Rosser

IN COLLABORATION WITH CORE

CHICAGO | 2025

© 2025 by Michael Hanegan and Chris Rosser

Extensive effort has gone into ensuring the reliability of the information in this book; however, the publisher makes no warranty, express or implied, with respect to the material contained herein.

ISBNs
979-8-89255-310-0 (paper)
979-8-89255-331-5 (PDF)

Library of Congress Cataloging-in-Publication Data

Names: Hanegan, Michael author | Rosser, Chris (Librarian) author
Title: Generative AI and libraries : claiming our place in the center of a shared future / Michael Hanegan and Chris Rosser.
Description: Chicago : ALA Editions in collaboration with Core, 2025. | Includes bibliographical references and index.
Identifiers: LCCN 2025017254 (print) | LCCN 2025017255 (ebook) | ISBN 9798892553100 paperback | ISBN 9798892553315 pdf
Subjects: LCSH: Artificial intelligence—Library applications | BISAC: LANGUAGE ARTS & DISCIPLINES / Library & Information Science / General
Classification: LCC Z678.93.A77 H36 2025 (print) | LCC Z678.93.A77 (ebook) | DDC 025.00685/63—dc23/eng/20250512
LC record available at https://lccn.loc.gov/2025017254
LC ebook record available at https://lccn.loc.gov/2025017255

Composition by Karen Sheets Design in the Skolar Latin, Source Sans, and Laski Slab typefaces. Cover design by Kim Hudgins.

♾ This paper meets the requirements of ANSI/NISO Z39.48-1992 (Permanence of Paper).

Printed in the United States of America
29 28 27 26 25   5 4 3 2 1

ALA Editions purchases fund advocacy, awareness, and accreditation programs for library professionals worldwide.

from Michael

To Krystal, my partner in life, who has never begrudged my love for books or ideas and who let me use her library card time and time again. To my kids, Samuel, Noah, and Jessi, who give me hope for the world that we can build and remind me to not take everything so seriously.

from Chris

To Heather and our children, Heath and Briar, Aunnah and Paige, and to my new friends Claude, Perplexity, and so many others, *imago Humana*, profound partners now for learning and work.

Contents

Introduction: Libraries Claim the Center   vii

PART I: FOUNDATIONS OF AI IN LIBRARIES

1. The Future of Learning and Work in Libraries   3
2. The Human-Centered Paradigm   17
3. Essential Concepts and Definitions   33

PART II: STRATEGIC IMPLEMENTATION OF AI IN LIBRARIES

4. The AI Integration Process   51
5. A Framework for AI Adoption   65
6. The Unseen Cost and Possibilities of AI Integration   79

PART III: THE FUTURE OF LIBRARIES IN THE AGE OF INTELLIGENCE

7. Metaliteracy: Exploring the Intersections of AI and the ACRL Framework   95
8. STACKS: An Approach for Learning, Problem-Solving, and Innovation with Generative AI   117

Conclusion: First Steps for Libraries in the Age of Intelligence   129

About the Authors   135

Index   137

Introduction
Libraries Claim the Center

A Japanese proverb—*en no shita no chikara mochi*—speaks of "the strong one under the floor"—a presence that upholds and sustains, and is invisible yet essential.[1] Throughout history, libraries have served as this foundational presence, supporting the intellectual infrastructure of communities, institutions, and societies. Today, as artificial intelligence reshapes how humans learn, work, and interact with information, libraries across the ecosystem—from public to academic, school to special libraries—must evolve from static support to dynamic influence. The strong one under the floor becomes the core, a center of gravity in the Age of Intelligence.

This evolution mirrors libraries' historical resilience through other technological transformations. When the codex (book) replaced the scroll as humanity's primary vessel for capturing and conveying knowledge, libraries adapted and thrived. We respond to disruption by reorganizing our spaces and practices to support new ways of accessing information. As we've returned to the *scroll*—now glowing screens instead of ancient parchment—libraries again demonstrate their capacity to embrace change while maintaining their essential character. Persistence through transformation is evidence of libraries' fundamental societal role in mediating technological capability and human-centered needs for the public good.

The rise of generative artificial intelligence (or generative AI) presents libraries with both unprecedented challenges and extraordinary opportunities. While this technological shift sparks varying reactions within our

{ vii }

profession—from cautious resistance to eager embrace—we maintain a grounded optimism about libraries' role in this transformation. This optimism stems not from blind faith in technology but from our profession's demonstrated capacity to guide technological change toward human flourishing. Across our ecosystem, libraries can and must claim a central position in AI integration by serving as trusted guides and ethical stewards. Our community-focused identities, our core mission of serving the public good, and our unrivaled capacities to provide instruction across the broadest range of literacies position us to shape responsible AI adoption. Libraries are not just relevant but essential in the Age of Intelligence. We're optimistic about libraries, AI, and the future of learning and work.

WHO WE ARE AND WHY WE OFFER THIS BOOK

As we begin, let us introduce ourselves and our work with generative AI. We're intentionally less formal and more conversational here than throughout the book; AI in libraries is, after all, a big and sometimes difficult conversation. We are first and foremost practitioners. We believe that theory and ethics are essential to our work, and we actively practice everything we unpack in this book. We work across education sectors and the larger library ecosystem to explore and enact human-centered approaches to generative AI and the work of teaching, learning, and service.

Chris is a first year and transfer experience librarian at an R1 institution working with students, faculty, and other librarians. Michael serves as an adjunct professor, advisor, and consultant across K–12, higher education, workforce development, and the library ecosystem. We each serve on the AI Impact Committee of our State Regents, offer workshops and presentations, and participate in various committees and events related to AI, libraries, learning, and work. After the publication of our white paper "Artificial Intelligence and the Future of Theological Education,"[2] our ideas, workshops, and teaching have helped shape thinking among librarians across various library types and beyond. This book is our next contribution to ongoing conversations about the place of AI in libraries and the place of the library in a world transformed by generative AI.

OUR ASSUMPTIONS: FOUNDATIONAL PRINCIPLES FOR THE AGE OF INTELLIGENCE

While our thinking will become more apparent as you read this book, we wanted to address directly and preemptively some of our working assumptions and commitments around generative artificial intelligence, and explain why some important conversations (in which we actively participate) are not included in this book. Let's begin with our assumptions.

Generative artificial intelligence is an arrival technology.

Do you remember the first time you purchased a cell phone or the time you transitioned to a smartphone? While perhaps necessitated by work or personal needs, or accelerated by peer pressure or personal interest and curiosity, your adoption and integration of this technology was an *elective* decision. Arrival technologies (like generative AI) are different.

An arrival technology fundamentally reshapes society regardless of individual choice or adoption. Unlike elective technologies—such as smartphones, which we can choose to use or not—arrival technologies transform the underlying fabric of how society functions. Consider electricity: Even if someone chose not to electrify their home, the electrification of their community dramatically altered commerce, social life, work, and daily routines. Similarly, the internet has become so deeply woven into our society's infrastructure that virtually no aspect of modern life remains untouched by its influence, whether one personally uses it or not.

Generative AI represents an arrival technology with an unprecedented speed of transformation. While the telephone took nearly 75 years to reach 100 million users and the internet took less than 7 years, ChatGPT achieved this milestone in just months.[3] Yet this rapid adoption speed tells only part of the story: What makes generative AI a true arrival technology is how it is fundamentally altering the nature of work, learning, and knowledge creation across society, affecting even those who never directly engage with it. Generative AI is already reshaping the way people learn, discover, and engage with information.

Ethical concerns about generative AI continue to rapidly evolve.

While we address various ethical concerns throughout this book, we're careful to place generative AI's challenges in context. Many issues attributed to

AI—from environmental impacts to privacy concerns—are extensions of long-standing societal challenges rather than entirely new problems. Libraries can play a crucial role by approaching these concerns with nuance, avoiding both uncritical enthusiasm and disproportionate anxiety about AI's effects. By maintaining this balanced perspective, we can better focus on how libraries can exercise agency in guiding AI development toward human flourishing.

The unprecedented pace of AI development challenges our traditional approaches to ethical reasoning and policy-making. Historically, humanity has navigated technological changes that progress incrementally, allowing time for careful consideration of their implications and the development of ethical frameworks. Generative AI's exponential rate of adoption has created a fundamentally different dynamic—one in which the window between identifying ethical concerns and needing practical responses continues to shrink.

This rapid evolution makes it crucial to focus on enduring ethical principles and adaptable frameworks rather than fixed positions. While specific ethical questions around AI are both urgent and essential, our response must be dynamic and evolving. Rather than offering static positions that may quickly become outdated, this book provides frameworks for ethical decision-making that can flex and scale up with technological advances. Consider, for example, how quickly our understanding of AI's environmental impact has evolved: A 2024 *Scientific Reports* study revealed that AI systems generate significantly lower carbon emissions than previously believed, with AI text generation producing 130–1,500 times less CO2e than human writers.[4] Yet even these findings represent a snapshot of rapidly improving efficiency. Our ethical frameworks must be robust enough to incorporate such evolving evidence while maintaining a focus on core principles of human and ecological flourishing.

There is effectively no opt-out strategy that is sustainable or effective.

We're not suggesting that there are not particular instances and applications where we must be critical about the implementation of generative AI. In fact, it is one of the primary arguments of this book that librarians and libraries are uniquely suited to help us think through these realities. However, we take for granted that this technology (and in more ways than most people realize) has already infiltrated and integrated into the world in which we live and work. Some may choose to not participate, but in much the same way that we no longer maintain library databases on physical cards in an analog card catalog or require that our holdings be in scroll format, we work in this book to help the library ecosystem navigate a world in which generative AI is already a fundamental part of the world as it really exists.

We are optimistic about the potential for generative AI to expand human flourishing but are conscious of how it could be leveraged to adversely shape our world.
We maintain measured optimism about generative AI's potential to advance human flourishing. In fields from medicine to environmental science, AI is already accelerating discovery and expanding our capacity for innovation. Dario Amodei's concept of the "compressed 21st century" captures this unprecedented acceleration: Developments that might have taken decades may now unfold within years, creating extraordinary opportunities for human progress and collective well-being.[5]

Yet this optimism is tempered by a clear-eyed recognition of the potential risks. Generative AI could exacerbate existing inequalities, trigger economic disruptions, enable sophisticated weapons development, amplify misinformation, and potentially diminish human agency and autonomy. These concerns aren't peripheral to our optimism; they're central to why libraries must claim a pivotal role in AI's development. As moral and ethical centers of gravity in our communities, libraries are uniquely positioned to guide AI implementation toward collective benefit while actively working to prevent or mitigate its harmful applications.

As we explore these opportunities and challenges, we believe it's essential to model the kind of transparency and thoughtful integration of AI tools that we advocate for libraries. Our own experience with AI tools in writing this book offers practical insights into how to approach human–AI collaboration while maintaining human agency and purpose.

OUR ACKNOWLEDGMENT AND APPROACH TO AI TOOLS

This book represents an interweaving of our work and the tools used for that work, some of which leverage generative AI in ways that were not even possible until very recently. We think it is important in these earliest days of the Age of Intelligence to speak openly and clearly about the paradigms and possibilities that are emerging for learning and innovation, and we hope that this project is a human-centered example of that kind of work. No material in this book is exclusively AI-generated; rather, the book in its entirety reflects collaboration with numerous tools employed for various purposes (this is what we refer to as "stacks" of tools).

We acknowledge using AI tools for the following:

Recording, transcription, and query. We used AI-powered videoconferencing tools to record, transcribe, and summarize our conversations; these transcriptions also provided the opportunity to search/query all of our conversations. (Specific tools include Zoom and Fathom.)

Organization and search within our own materials. In the last two years, we have offered hundreds of presentations, meetings, and trainings with thousands of participants, both individually and together, and thus have an extensive corpus of slide decks, notes, manuscripts, and video and audio recordings *of our own work*. We have used AI tools and integrations to navigate and manage all this content, to locate specific materials (e.g., "that one time I talked about [fill in the blank] . . . but I can't remember which presentation it was . . ."). (Specific tools include Notion, Canva, Sana, Claude, Fathom, NotebookLM, Gemini for Google Workspace, Perplexity, and ChatGPT.)

Ideation. We used tools and integrations to help us organize, rearrange, and clarify our ideas. We did this through practices like taking unstructured research and notes and asking the tools to categorize and align the materials we had created. We would "pressure test" some ideas and metaphors, asking for guidance and awareness of blind spots or inadequacies in metaphors and frameworks. We leveraged these tools and integrations to synergize and synthesize our reflection and conversation (often across many months) into a more actionable and interpretable expression. (Specific tools include Claude, Perplexity, ChatGPT, Gemini, Sana, Fathom, Notion, and NotebookLM.)

Grammar and flow. We leveraged tools that are integrated into the writing software that we used for the various parts of our work. We deployed these tools for grammar, spelling, and flow. All content and ideas were original, and changes were never more than a word or two, or accepting guidance that edits should be made. (Specific tools include Gemini with Google Docs, Grammarly, Notion, ButterDocs, and Microsoft Word with Co-Pilot.)

This acknowledgment itself exemplifies the approach we advocate: Transparency about AI involvement, while recognizing that new frameworks for understanding learning, thinking, research, authorship, and attribution are needed as human-AI collaboration becomes increasingly sophisticated and intertwined.

OUR APPROACH: BUILDING FRAMEWORKS FOR LIBRARIES AS CENTERS OF GRAVITY

This transparent approach to AI integration exemplifies a key theme of this book: Libraries must lead by example in demonstrating how to thoughtfully incorporate AI while staying true to core values and human-centered purposes. To help libraries claim their central role in AI development and adoption, we must first establish foundational principles that can withstand rapid technological change. Like gravity itself, these principles must be both constant and dynamic, providing stability while enabling movement and growth. This shapes our approach in this book.

We provide theory and frameworks because most concrete AI applications are still emerging.

While you'll find practical applications throughout this book, our primary focus is on developing robust frameworks and strengthening the core values that will guide libraries through this technological transformation. We make this choice deliberately, recognizing that specific AI tools and applications will evolve, but fundamental principles will remain essential. This theoretical foundation serves three key purposes.

First, focusing too quickly on AI's practical applications can create a false sense of mastery. Consider learning to drive: Success in an empty parking lot doesn't prepare one for navigating rush-hour traffic on the expressway. Similarly, we've observed from working with many practitioners, that rushing to implement AI tools without understanding core principles often leads to superficial adoption rather than meaningful integration.

Second, the capabilities of AI tools are expanding at an unpredictable and unprecedented pace. In our teaching and presentations, we regularly encounter this acceleration—for instance, Michael recently planned a class assignment around a cutting-edge AI model, only to find it replaced by a more advanced version within fifteen minutes of the class ending. Such rapid advances have become routine, and we expect this pace to accelerate even more in the coming years.

Finally, the enduring strength of libraries lies not in mastering specific technologies but in our fundamental values and expertise—the qualities that have always made us "the strong one under the floor." Our approach emphasizes these core strengths because they become even more crucial in a world transformed by AI. While technologies evolve continuously, our professional values and expertise provide the stable foundation needed to guide their thoughtful implementation.

A BRIEF WORD ABOUT CLAIMING THE CENTER

Throughout this book, we explore how libraries, librarians, and the library ecosystem function as gravitational forces that can help shape our collective future, particularly as we navigate the transformative impact of generative AI. When we speak of "claiming the center," we emphasize three key principles.

1. Libraries' values and expertise are vital to our shared future.

We believe that the core values and expertise of librarians and the library ecosystem are essential to the vitality, well-being, and future of the human family. These foundational strengths—our commitment to equity, privacy, intellectual freedom, and informed decision-making—become even more crucial as AI reshapes how we learn, work, and interact. Rather than being left behind, these values must be amplified and made more visible in public discourse.

2. Claiming the center means stepping forward to serve.

As we witness the fundamental reshaping of human learning, work, and the social fabric, libraries have a unique responsibility to step forward. This isn't about asserting dominance or claiming territory, but about actively embracing our role as trusted guides and ethical stewards. Just as we've been "the strong one under the floor," we must now visibly help guide our communities toward collective flourishing in this transformative moment.

3. The center is not about self-importance or power but about orientation, connection, and impact.

Being central doesn't mean controlling power or commanding attention. Instead, like gravity itself, libraries serve as a connecting force that both supports and energizes the communities around us. We aim to be a dynamic presence that helps guide technological progress toward human-centered outcomes.

We understand that it doesn't always feel like libraries have sufficient agency to influence change. Undoubtedly there are times when we feel overwhelmed, marginalized, or powerless in the face of so many challenges to cultivating and sustaining a world that is good for everyone, not just the few. Yet even in constrained circumstances, every instance of libraries exercising agency—whether through small daily choices or larger institutional decisions—adds strength to our collective influence. When individual libraries assert their values and expertise, even in limited ways, they reinforce the entire ecosystem's capacity for positive change. We recognize that this vision may seem ambitious, particularly when every library faces its own challenges and constraints. Yet we believe libraries' potential to shape positive technological change remains largely untapped. We offer this book as timely guidance for libraries to embrace their vital role in this profound transformation. There is urgent work ahead, and we hope this book offers a robust and constructive place to begin.

WHAT TO EXPECT IN THIS BOOK

This book provides frameworks for libraries to embrace their role as centers of gravity in the Age of Intelligence. We organize our approach in three parts:

- **Part I (chapters 1-3)** establishes libraries as centers of gravity, provides ethical foundations, and develops essential concepts for understanding AI's impact.
- **Part II (chapters 4-6)** offers practical models for evaluating and implementing AI tools thoughtfully and effectively.
- **Part III (chapters 7-9)** explores AI literacy as an expression of metaliteracy, introducing seven frames for instruction and our "gravitational model" for learning.

Our vision requires collective action. Through professional organizations like the American Library Association and grassroots collaborations, libraries must work together to shape policy and practice at all levels. This collaborative approach unites what we call the "prophets and priests" of technological change—those driving innovation and those protecting core values—in the service of thoughtful AI integration. Through our collective strength, we can ensure that AI development advances human dignity, intellectual freedom, and equitable access to knowledge.

The multiple literacies that have long been central to librarianship are precisely what society needs to navigate this technological transformation. Just as the Japanese proverb speaks of "the strong one under the floor," libraries have always provided essential support for human learning and development. But in this Age of Intelligence, we must increasingly evolve from invisible support to visible guidance—from foundation to center of gravity.

We claim the center not through assertions of power but through service to our communities. As centers of gravity in an AI-enhanced world, we can shape technological change toward flourishing for all. The future we envision begins with the choices we make today. Now is our moment to claim the center.

NOTES

1. 縁の下の力持ち, translated here as "the strong one under the floor," refers to a person who consistently serves others without acknowledgment of that person's dedicated service. In our experience, libraries are often the *en no shita no chikara mochi* serving institutions, communities, and society.

2. Michael Hanegan and Chris Rosser, "Artificial Intelligence and the Future of Theological Education, Version 2.0," June 12, 2024, https://bit.ly/theological-education-and-ai.

3. Christof Ebert and Panos Louridas, "Generative AI for Software Practitioners," *IEEE Software* 40, no. 4 (July 2023): 30–38, https://doi.org/10.1109/MS.2023.3265877.

4. Bill Tomlinson et al., "The Carbon Emissions of Writing and Illustrating Are Lower for AI Than for Humans," *Scientific Reports* 14, no. 1 (February 14, 2024): 3732, https://doi.org/10.1038/s41598-024-54271-x.

5. Dario Amodei, "Machines of Loving Grace: How AI Could Transform the World for the Better," October 2024, https://darioamodei.com/machines-of-loving-grace.

PART I

Foundations of AI in Libraries

1

The Future of Learning and Work in Libraries

What goes up must come down. This familiar adage captures gravity's fundamental nature: a force that both stabilizes and governs movement. Right now, at the dawn of generative artificial intelligence, everything feels up in the air. Questions about AI's impact on learning, work, and human agency seem to multiply daily. Who or what will stabilize and guide this technological momentum? We assert that libraries must become centers of gravity in the Age of Intelligence.[1] Libraries must provide stability and momentum—anchoring communities in enduring values while energizing movement toward desired futures. This dual role transforms libraries from static support structures into dynamic centers of influence, actively shaping how AI develops and impacts our communities.

The trajectory of artificial intelligence itself demonstrates this gravitational principle. While the initial shock of generative AI's emergence has begun to settle, fundamental questions about hallucinations, plagiarism, job displacement, and copyright implications continue to demand thoughtful engagement and evolving solutions. Environmental concerns about AI's significant energy footprint remain central to discussions about responsible implementation, pushing us toward more sustainable approaches. As these challenges mature from acute anxieties into sustained areas for practical action and policy development, we observe that *what goes up must come down*—not in the sense of diminishing importance but in the transformation of abstract concerns

> Libraries can "claim the center" not as passive responders to AI development, but as active shapers of its trajectory through our unique combination of community connections, values orientation, and deep expertise. Our collective agency creates sustained upward force.

into concrete areas for intervention and improvement.

Yet, concerning our capacity to influence this moment, libraries can harness this gravitational metaphor differently: While individual enthusiasm and energy naturally ebb and flow, our collective agency creates a sustained upward force. Together, libraries across our ecosystem can maintain the momentum needed to shape AI implementation in libraries toward human and ecological flourishing. Together, *what goes up can stay*. Libraries across all contexts can claim a central position as trusted guides in the Age of Intelligence, leveraging our community-focused mission, our unique community connections, and our expertise in supporting multiple literacies to champion responsible innovation that serves the public good.

LIBRARIES AS STABILIZING, CONNECTING, AND ENERGIZING FORCES

Libraries first provide this sustained upward force through their fundamental role as *stabilizing institutions*. While technological change creates constant turbulence, libraries anchor their communities through an enduring commitment to core values and ethical principles. We provide temporal stability by preserving institutional and cultural memory, and we provide communal stability through our sustained presence and fundamental services. We provide technological stability through our thoughtful evaluation and curation of emerging technologies, our advocacy for sustainable practices, and our stewardship of responsible adoption. And finally, we provide informational and formational stability—what we might call (in)formational stability—through the literacies and durable skills we develop and protect. This dual work of informing and forming our constituencies for the public good is explicit in our core values as libraries.[2] Libraries' stabilizing force doesn't resist change but ensures that transformation serves human needs and values. Like gravity, libraries can help create the stable environment necessary for communities to thrive amid technological change.

Building on this stable foundation, libraries serve as *connecting forces*, bringing diverse stakeholders into meaningful collaboration and innovation. Libraries create and mediate vital connections throughout the information ecosystem. We connect locally in our communities, nationally through our professional associations, and globally through our shared commitment to human flourishing. This connecting force operates on multiple levels:

- Within our ecosystem, it unites public, academic, school, and special libraries through shared values and common purpose. Though our contexts differ, we are all fundamentally libraries and librarians, drawing strength from our collective identity and shared ethical commitments. This unity amplifies our collective influence, enabling us to speak with one voice[3] on crucial AI development and implementation issues.
- Beyond our walls, we connect diverse stakeholders who might otherwise remain isolated: We connect practitioners with researchers, developers with users, policy-makers with communities, and technologies with human needs. Our unique position—present in nearly every community, institution, and level of society—enables us to influence conversations about AI ranging from local computer labs to global policy forums. Perhaps most importantly, we connect the past and the future, bridging traditional knowledge practices with emerging technologies. This temporal connection opens the possibility that our leadership in modeling AI adoption will benefit from established wisdom while embracing innovation.

Finally, libraries act as *energizing forces*, converting potential into purposeful movement toward the futures we envision. Just as gravity transforms potential energy into kinetic motion, libraries transform technological possibility into meaningful change. This is not passive influence but active agency, a deliberate exercise of our gravitational power to shape how AI develops within and impacts our communities. Through advocacy, instruction, and leadership, we energize institutions, communities, and society to move toward policies and practices that serve human and ecological flourishing. The moment for this energizing force is now. If libraries are to claim the center in an AI-enhanced world, we must recognize and embrace

> As centers of gravity, libraries stabilize, connect, and energize, three forces that characterize our influence.

our capacity to influence change. Our stabilizing presence and connecting power create the conditions; our energizing force provides the momentum. Together, these gravitational forces enable libraries to guide AI development toward the futures we imagine and the flourishing we seek.

These gravitational forces—stabilizing, connecting, and energizing—position libraries to capably respond to profound changes in how humans learn, work, and engage with information. As we examine the shifting information landscape, we see why libraries must claim this central role. Our move to become dynamic centers of gravity is both an opportunity and a responsibility driven by accelerating technological and social change.

GRAVITATIONAL AGENCY: EXERTING INFLUENCE ACROSS THE LIBRARY ECOSYSTEM

This vision of libraries as centers of gravity requires us to recognize and exercise our agency—our capacity to influence and shape AI development and integration at multiple levels. Our gravitational influence operates across three interconnected spheres: personal, institutional, and ecosystem.

At the personal level, individual librarians exercise gravitational agency through their daily choices and interactions. When a librarian thoughtfully integrates AI tools into their workflows, provides guidance on ethical AI use, or models critical engagement with AI technologies, they exert a stabilizing and energizing influence on their immediate environment. Personal agency manifests when we choose to develop our own AI literacy, when we advocate for thoughtful approaches in meetings and working groups, and when we create instructional moments that develop critical AI understanding in our colleagues and the people we serve. These individual actions may seem small, but like planetary bodies exerting their gravitational pull, each librarian contributes to the cumulative gravitational field of our profession.

Institutional agency emerges as libraries develop strategic approaches to AI adoption and education. When libraries establish committees to evaluate AI tools, help the institution to create policies that guide ethical implementation or develop instructional programs that enhance community AI literacy, they exercise collective agency that shapes the library's approach and the broader institutional culture around AI. By curating AI resources, creating spaces for community dialogue, and forming strategic partnerships with vendors to influence product development, libraries fulfill their role as centers of gravity within their communities and organizations. Importantly, institutional agency leverages the connections that libraries maintain across both internal and external stakeholders, enabling them to bring together perspectives that might otherwise remain isolated.

The ecosystem level represents our broadest sphere of influence, where libraries collectively exert gravitational force through professional organizations, cross-institutional collaborations, and unified advocacy. When libraries speak with one voice on crucial AI development and policy issues, they transform individual actions into coordinated movements that shape public understanding and regulatory approaches. Through organizations like the American Library Association (ALA), libraries can amplify their gravitational influence, creating standards, sharing resources, and advocating for ethical AI development and deployment that serve the public good. This collective agency enables libraries to influence technological trajectories far beyond their individual or institutional reach.

These three spheres of agency—personal, institutional, and ecosystem—are not separate but deeply interconnected. Like nested gravitational fields, each level influences and strengthens the others. When individual librarians exercise personal agency, they enhance their institution's capacity for collective action. When institutions collaborate, they strengthen the library ecosystem's ability to shape and reshape broader social and technological change. And when the ecosystem explicitly and unapologetically exerts its collective influence, it empowers individual librarians to take more effective action in their local contexts.

By recognizing and intentionally exercising our agency across these spheres, libraries can accept responsibility and enact change as centers of gravity in the Age of Intelligence—not through assertions of power but through the consistent application of our gravitational influence to guide AI development toward human and ecological flourishing.

CLAIMING THE CENTER IN A SHIFTING INFORMATION LANDSCAPE

Libraries have long transcended any initial role as static repositories of knowledge. With each technological revolution—from the printing press to the internet—libraries have evolved to meet new challenges while maintaining their essential character.⁴ The rise of the internet prompted libraries to expand beyond physical collections and develop crucial frameworks like information literacy and later metaliteracy to help communities navigate an increasingly complex digital landscape. These frameworks have empowered learners to use new tools and think critically about how information is created, shared, and used.

> In all contexts across the library ecosystem, libraries can claim the center by serving as trusted guides and ethical stewards in the Age of Intelligence, leveraging our unique position as community-focused institutions to promote responsible AI adoption that serves the public good.

Generative artificial intelligence (GenAI) presents an acceleration and extension of this journey and, along with it, an unprecedented opportunity. The rapid pace of AI development demands that libraries once again move quickly to adapt and expand their gravitational influence. Just as information literacy became crucial for navigating the internet age, navigating GenAI—as a kind of metaliteracy—is fast becoming essential for thriving in the Age of Intelligence. This capacity isn't only about using AI tools; it's about understanding their implications, engaging with them ethically, and shaping their development to serve human needs.

Yet this moment differs from previous technological transitions. The speed and scope of the advances in GenAI, combined with its emerging impact on how humans learn and work, demand that libraries do more than adapt—they must actively claim a central position as meaningful partners in emerging conversations about GenAI's development, adoption, and use.

The concept of libraries "claiming the center" in GenAI development and adoption is particularly apt given libraries' unique position as trusted, mission-driven institutions that bridge knowledge, technology, and community needs. In claiming the center, libraries can leverage the following key aspects:

1. *Historical precedent and expertise*: Libraries have long served as mediators between emerging technologies and public understanding. Libraries have been teaching critical evaluation, information synthesis, and the ethical use of information for decades, which positions them as key providers of the skills and literacies needed for proficiency with GenAI tools.

2. *Social and institutional positioning*: Libraries occupy a unique space as noncommercial, public-interest institutions with deep community connections. Academic libraries exist as co-curricular, interdepartmental hubs or nexus points that are central to campus connectedness. Many libraries serve as vital "third places"—those essential community spaces beyond home and work where people gather, connect, and build community.[5] This positioning allows them to serve as brokers in conversations about AI, free from the profit motives that might influence corporate actors and from the political pressures that affect government entities. The public perception of libraries as meaningful providers of skill development and AI literacy takes on additional significance at a time when libraries face increasing challenges, including rising anti-library sentiment and attempts at censorship in American society. Positioning libraries as essential guides in AI adoption and literacy reinforces their fundamental value to communities.
3. *Adaptive implementation*: Recognizing that "claiming the center" will manifest differently across contexts is crucial. A rural public library might focus on basic AI literacy and practical applications for its community, while an academic research library might engage with advanced AI research and policy discussions. The diversity of contexts in which libraries exist magnifies their potential for transformative influence.

As stewards of information and knowledge, libraries seek neither to own nor control the center; rather, we assume our crucial role as centers of stability, influence, and instruction. In whatever context, libraries claim the center by providing:

- *Stability* that grounds technological change in ethical principles
- *Influence* that shapes policy and implementation
- *Instruction* that develops critical AI literacy across our communities

The emergence of generative AI is transforming fundamental aspects of how knowledge is created, shared, and preserved. Libraries have always been more than information custodians; we actively participate in knowledge creation through instruction, research support, and community engagement. As AI becomes a potential partner in knowledge creation, libraries must help their communities navigate new questions. How do we evaluate AI-enhanced research and creative works? What does authority mean when content is co-created with AI? How do we preserve and provide access to AI-generated materials while maintaining intellectual integrity?

These questions extend to curation, traditionally a cornerstone of library services. Curation in the Age of Intelligence involves selecting, evaluating, and organizing information and tools while mediating the complex relationship between human and machine intelligence. Libraries must develop frameworks for evaluating AI tools and outputs, supporting ethical co-creation practices, preserving the provenance of AI-enhanced work, and ensuring transparency in how knowledge is produced. This evolution in knowledge creation and curation exemplifies why libraries must claim the center of AI integration. Our expertise in organizing, evaluating, and providing access to information becomes even more crucial as the boundaries between human- and machine-generated content blur. By exercising our gravitational influence—stabilizing through ethical frameworks, connecting diverse stakeholders, and energizing thoughtful innovation and instruction—libraries can help ensure that AI enhances rather than diminishes the integrity of knowledge creation.

As these shifts in knowledge creation and curation demonstrate, we stand at a critical juncture. GenAI's changes to learning and work aren't merely technological shifts but represent fundamental transformations in how humans create, share, and apply knowledge. To understand why libraries must now claim the center, we will first examine some larger trends and trajectories reshaping our world. These patterns reveal the urgency of our moment and the unique value of libraries' gravitational influence in guiding technological change for the public good.

LARGER TRENDS AND TRAJECTORIES

As centers of gravity in the Age of Intelligence, libraries must navigate several interconnected trends that are transforming how we learn and work.[6] These aren't gradual shifts but powerful forces that are rapidly reshaping society's relationship with knowledge and technology. Our gravitational influence becomes crucial as these trends accelerate and intersect, creating unprecedented challenges, disruptions, and opportunities for libraries to guide the future.

Skills-Based Economy

The shift toward a skills-based economy exerts its own gravitational pull, fundamentally changing how people learn and work. Traditional credentials increasingly complement rather than dominate hiring and promotion decisions, while continuous skills development becomes essential for career sustainability. Through their gravitational influence, libraries can help communities navigate this transition by providing access to learning resources, validating skill development, and creating spaces where traditional and emerging competencies intersect. Our role is to ensure that this shift advances equitably and ethically.

Libraries across our ecosystem are uniquely positioned to support skill development for diverse learners. Academic libraries can partner with faculty to integrate crucial digital and AI competencies into curricula. Public libraries can provide community access to learning platforms and skill-development resources. School libraries can prepare students for future careers by fostering technological and critical thinking skills. Special libraries can help professionals adapt to changing industry demands. Together, we can (and will) create a comprehensive support system for continuous learning and skill enhancement.

Decentralized Learning

Decentralized learning transforms how knowledge flows through society. Learning now happens everywhere, through multiple channels and modalities, with GenAI accelerating this dispersion. Libraries serve as crucial nodes or hubs in this distributed network, providing access to resources and helping learners integrate knowledge from diverse sources. Libraries as a connecting force can bring coherence to fragmented learning experiences, while our stability helps ensure accessibility in an increasingly decentralized education system.

Libraries play an essential role in democratizing access to decentralized learning opportunities. We bridge the digital divide by providing technology access and the guidance needed to use it effectively. From high-speed internet and computer workstations to AI tools and digital learning platforms, libraries help ensure these resources reach all community members, not just those who can afford them. This commitment to equitable access becomes even more crucial as AI tools become increasingly central to learning and work.

Up-skilling and Re-skilling

The continuous cycle of up-skilling and re-skilling reflects an economy in constant evolution. As AI automates certain tasks while creating new opportunities, workers must regularly enhance their existing skills and develop new ones. Libraries' presence in communities and institutions positions us to drive and support this ongoing transformation. We provide resources for skill development and guidance in connecting skills with jobs and how to acquire them both ethically and effectively.

As GenAI reshapes the employment landscape, a certain level of literacy and proficiency becomes crucial for workforce success. Employers across sectors are seeking workers who can thoughtfully engage with AI tools and systems. Libraries must position themselves at the center of these developments, helping communities acquire these high-demand skills while maintaining critical awareness of AI's implications. Our instructional role extends beyond teaching tool use to fostering the deeper understanding needed for meaningful human–AI collaboration. Libraries level up communities.

Acceleration and Expansion of Automation

Finally, automation's rapid advancement into traditional work roles demands thoughtful responses and adaptation. Rather than simply accepting automation or reflexively resisting it, libraries can guide their communities toward meaningful human–AI synergy. Our gravitational influence helps stakeholders navigate the renegotiation of roles between humans and machines, helping ensure that automation enhances rather than diminishes human capability and agency.

How Libraries Can Lead the Way

This navigation requires imagination and purposeful action. Libraries must help communities reimagine how human experience and expertise can complement rather than compete with GenAI capabilities. We can model this approach through our services, demonstrating how this integration enhances rather than replaces human judgment and interaction. By exercising agency in how we implement this technology, we show our communities paths toward productive human–AI partnerships that preserve and amplify our humanity.

These interconnected trends and trajectories don't demand a fundamental transformation of libraries but rather an evolutionary adaptation of our services. Across our ecosystem, libraries must thoughtfully evolve how we support learning and work while maintaining our core mission and values. This evolution positions us to actively shape these changes through shared agency, influence, and instruction.

To exercise our influence, libraries need a shared grammar for understanding, navigating, and implementing AI across our ecosystem. The remainder of this book attempts to provide this foundation, offering frameworks and approaches for libraries to claim their central role in shaping technological progress and adoption that serve human and ecological flourishing.

THE ENHANCED LIBRARY

While these trends and trajectories create challenges, they reveal libraries' enhanced value and amplified purpose in the Age of Intelligence. As technological change accelerates, our fundamental work as libraries and librarians becomes more complex, urgent, and vital to human flourishing. We see this enhancement across several dimensions, as discussed in the following subsections.

Enhanced Complexity

Libraries have always navigated multifaceted challenges, but generative AI adds new layers of complexity to our core work. We must now consider the implications of human-AI collaboration in research and learning, develop frameworks for evaluating AI-generated content, and create policies that promote ethical use. This increased complexity provides a matrix in which libraries can demonstrate their unique capability to bring clarity and purpose to technological change.

Enhanced Urgency

The rapid development of generative AI creates unprecedented urgency for thoughtful integration and ethical guidance. Libraries cannot wait to see how this development unfolds—we must actively shape its trajectory today. This urgency extends beyond our walls to the communities we serve, who need immediate support in navigating GenAI's impact on learning, work, and daily life. Our role in this work becomes not just important but essential.

Enhanced Value
As information landscapes grow more complex, libraries' role as trusted guides becomes increasingly crucial. Our expertise in evaluating information, promoting ethical use, and fostering critical thinking takes on new significance. We provide access to AI tools and the frameworks needed to use them thoughtfully and effectively. This enhanced value emerges from our unique position at the intersection of technology, information, and human needs.

Enhanced Agency
Perhaps most importantly, this moment reveals libraries' capacity to actively shape technological change. We are not passive observers but influential agents in determining how generative AI will be integrated into our communities and institutions. This framing gives libraries both agency and responsibility in the Age of Intelligence while also acknowledging the very real challenges that need to be addressed.

These enhancements in complexity, urgency, value, and agency demand new ways of thinking about and discussing AI integration. To fully realize our enhanced role and amplified purpose, we need a shared vocabulary and shared frameworks for engaging the work ahead.

DEVELOPING A SHARED GRAMMAR

Just as gravity provides a fundamental grammar for understanding motion and relationships in the physical universe, libraries need a shared language for understanding and shaping our approach to generative AI. This book offers not a comprehensive manual but an essential grammar, providing foundational concepts, imaginative frames, and practical models for thinking about ethics, adoption, instruction, and library evolution in the Age of Intelligence.

This basic grammar serves multiple purposes. It helps us articulate challenges and opportunities, envision possibilities, and coordinate responses across our ecosystem. It enables meaningful dialogue between what we call the "prophets and priests" of technological change—those who push for innovation and those who continuously point us back to our core values. Most importantly, the grammar provides a foundation for collective action.

While individual libraries and librarians can and must act locally, our most significant influence emerges through collective agency. Professional organizations like ALA become crucial amplifiers of our collective influence, enabling us to speak with one voice on crucial issues of AI development and implementation. Through these associations, we transform individual actions into coordinated movements that shape policy, practice, and public understanding.

In these earliest days of generative AI, we could throw up our hands in resignation or anxiety about the changes ahead. But this is not the librarian way. Instead of raising our hands in frustration or defeat, we should use them to do the vital work before us. We should reach out to connect with colleagues across our ecosystem. We should ground ourselves in our enduring values while reaching toward the futures we envision. We must get to work.

This is our moment to claim the center and become the gravitational force guiding the ongoing impact of generative AI in the direction of human flourishing. Through a shared language, collective action, and purposeful evolution, libraries can ensure that technological progress serves the public good. The grammar provided in this book offers a place to begin.

NOTES

1. We employ the phrase "Age of Intelligence" throughout this book as shorthand for this period marked by the emergence of generative AI, a technology with capabilities that match or exceed human performance in various domains of work, learning, and knowledge creation. Our use of the phrase "Age of Intelligence" should not indicate certainty that the world has generally entered a new era or adopted a new governing paradigm; rather, we use the phrase to refer to the realities of work and learning that are being transformed and empowered by GenAI. The term echoes Sam Altman's controversial 2024 essay "The Intelligence Age," which positions AI as the defining technological leap of our era. See Sam Altman, "The Intelligence Age," September 23, 2024, https://ia.samaltman.com. For a helpful critique, see Luke Munn, "It's 'the Intelligence Age,' Say Tech Titans—But Information Will Not Save Us," *The Conversation*, November 14, 2024, https://theconversation.com/friday-essay-its-the-intelligence-age-say-tech-titans-but-information-will-not-save-us-243158.

2. We employ the construct *(in)formation* as a shorthand for conveying the informational and formational work of librarianship among our communities across the library ecosystem as explicit in our core values: "Libraries are an essential public good and are fundamental institutions in democratic societies. Library workers provide the highest service levels to create informed, connected, educated, and empowered communities." See American Library Association, "Core Values of Librarianship," www.ala.org/advocacy/advocacy/intfreedom/corevalues.

3. For crucial guidance on speaking "with one voice" across library types, see Dorcas Hand, Sara Kelly Johns, Michelle Robertson, and Eryn Duffee, *Strengthening Library Ecosystems: Collaborate for Advocacy and Impact* (Chicago: American Library Association, 2024). See also the resources provided by the American Library Association, "ALA Ecosystem Initiative, One Voice: Building a Strong Library Ecosystem," www.ala.org/advocacy/ala-ecosystem-initiative.

4. See the engaging history of libraries from ancient times to the present in Andrew Pettegree and Arthur der Weduwen, *The Library: A Fragile History* (New York: Basic Books, 2023).

5. Much has been said about libraries as "third places" since Ray Oldenburg coined the term in 1989. See his reprinted work in Ray Oldenburg, *The Great Good Place: Cafés, Coffee Shops, Bookstores, Bars, Hair Salons, and Other Hangouts at the Heart of a Community* (New York: Marlowe, 1999).

6. Among numerous discussions of how AI is transforming work within and outside of libraries, see World Economic Forum, "Future of Jobs Report," 2025, https://reports.weforum.org/docs/WEF_Future_of_Jobs_Report_2025.pdf. See also American Library Association, "Artificial Intelligence," Center for the Future of Libraries, www.ala.org/future/trends/artificialintelligence.

2

The Human-Centered Paradigm

Now is a moment of unprecedented opportunity for human–AI synergy, where libraries emerge as vital centers of gravity in our evolving information ecosystem. This positioning is not a revolution but a natural evolution of libraries' enduring societal role. As described in chapter 1, libraries act as gravitational forces, gathering and organizing knowledge, connecting people, motivating change, and sustaining our intellectual ecosystem. Within a gravitational system, gravity simultaneously stabilizes and generates motion; similarly, within society, libraries exert a stabilizing yet generative influence that shapes how knowledge, technology, and human needs interact and align.

To understand this positioning more deeply, we draw inspiration from Japanese philosophy and language. Libraries embody "the strong one under the floor"—providing foundational support that often goes unnoticed yet remains essential—and the dynamic concept of *aida*, or "betweenness." *Aida* is a profound Japanese concept that recognizes the gap or space between one and another as a creative emptiness enabling relationships and interactions.[1] Below and between, libraries function as a generative human and intellectual infrastructure—dynamically weaving connections, bridging diverse perspectives, and catalyzing intellectual and social transformation.

In the Age of Intelligence, libraries operate through two critical spatial planes that reveal their transformative potential: *between* and *below*. These modes are dynamic mechanisms of technological and social mediation.

{ 17 }

Between: As generative, relational spaces, libraries actively mediate several critical intersections:

- Technology encounters human agency.
- Innovation dialogues with ethical consideration.
- Individual learning connects with collective wisdom.
- Institutional goals align with broader societal needs.

These intersections are charged with dynamic potential; *influence* is a function of our capacity to create connections and facilitate meaningful interactions within these spaces.

Below: As the stabilizing core of our knowledge ecosystem, libraries provide:

- Foundational scaffolding for AI literacy
- Stable infrastructure for AI implementation
- Preservation of and access to knowledge across generations
- Ethical frameworks that center human and ecological flourishing

Our positioning—between and below—creates an unseen but persistent gravitational field of influence. It provides the stability necessary for thoughtful AI integration while enabling the dynamic movement essential for innovation and growth.

Libraries have always centered human *being* in the world, serving the people of our communities, institutions, schools, and societies. When we speak of human-centered AI in libraries, we're not claiming human supremacy or exceptionalism. Instead, we're acknowledging something simpler and more profound: *Humans have agency in shaping how AI develops and impacts our world.*[2] Because we have agency—individual and collective—we determine our agency's end or aim. We choose the human and ecological flourishing that are explicit in librarianship's core values and ethics as our unapologetic objective. Agency, emerging from our unique position between and below, isn't a mark of privilege but a source of power and profound obligation.

> **A human-centered paradigm means recognizing that humans have agency in shaping how AI develops and impacts our world.**

FROM EXCEPTIONALISM TO OBLIGATION: A HUMAN-CENTERED PARADIGM

As we enter an unprecedented era of AI development, libraries' foundational position creates both opportunity and responsibility. The literacies central to librarianship and the durable skills these provide are crucial for the future of human learning and work. By leveraging our position below and between, we can claim the center of AI discussions and decisions not through privilege but through obligation—an obligation to ensure that AI contributes to the enhancement of our shared life.

To fulfill this obligation thoughtfully and systematically, we will examine AI integration through three interconnected dimensions that reflect our unique positioning.

1. *"In the World": Practical Implementation.* This dimension reveals AI as a collaborative partner. Here, technology becomes an extension of human creativity, amplifying our capabilities while preserving the nuances of human intuition. Implementation centers not on efficiency and productivity but on enhancing human potential and flourishing. Human–AI synergies "in the world" envision AI as

    » An amplifier of human expertise, creativity, and understanding
    » A bridge connecting diverse knowledge systems and domains
    » A catalyst for unprecedented human potential

2. *"Of the World": Existential Implications.* Here, we explore the profound social and ecological fabric into which AI is woven. When we consider AI "of the world," we're examining how AI affects the very nature of human *being* and *doing*, particularly its potential to exacerbate existing challenges or create new ones.[3] This requires a creative tension between AI's capacity to enhance human flourishing and its potential to diminish flourishing through inequities, environmental impacts, job displacement, and other concerns. Here, AI becomes a mirror revealing our deepest social complexities. We consider how technological systems

    » Expose hidden or under-recognized social fault lines
    » Challenge power hierarchies and problematic notions of identity
    » Reshape the very fabric of human connections with others and with our environments

3. *"For the World": Transformative Purpose.* The third dimension transcends instrumental thinking. Here, AI becomes a collective endeavor, a collaborative technology designed not only to solve problems but one with which we imagine new possibilities for human and ecological flourishing. As we consider AI synergies "for the world," we focus on the *ethical horizon*—not some distant future, but the edge where today transitions into tomorrow. This orientation empowers us to take meaningful action in the present moment while maintaining clarity about who we are and who we are working to become. This dimension imagines AI as a collaborative partner for

   » Reimagining collective potential
   » Bridging systemic divides, ensuring equitable access and representation
   » Cultivating an ecological imagination and prioritizing sustainability

The "in, of, and for the world" framework provides a thoughtful approach to AI ethics that addresses three crucial dimensions of engagement: practical implementation ("in the world"; how we thoughtfully integrate AI into our daily work), existential implications ("of the world"; how AI affects human dignity, formation, and community), and transformative purpose ("for the world"; how AI can serve libraries' broader mission of serving communities). This three-fold framework incorporates practical, formational, and missional aspects while providing a structure for moving from concrete AI applications to more profound questions of purpose and impact.

These dimensions guide our evaluation of AI integration through two fundamental questions that embody our commitment to human-centered AI: What does AI do *to* human *being* in the world? What does AI do *for* human *being* in the world?

This framework supports our core belief: *A human-centered approach to AI means recognizing and claiming human agency in governing AI development and integration.* This paradigm acknowledges our responsibility to shape AI for our collective benefit, ensuring it is designed and implemented with intention and ethical consideration. It means *purposefully* integrating AI not as an end in itself but as a tool to enhance human and ecological flourishing.

Certainly, we might also ask: What do *libraries* do to and for human *being* in the world? This fundamental question ignites agency and shapes our deepest decisions about service and advocacy. Technology is not something that happens to us but a collaborative space we continuously shape and by which we are transformed. Emerging from our position between and below, libraries can actively model AI integration that enhances human capabilities and cultivates collective flourishing.

THE ETHICAL HORIZON: WHERE TODAY MEETS TOMORROW

The advent of AI reveals a transformational landscape where fears and hopes converge at the edge of possibility. While some envision reformation, others see a renaissance, and many fear disruption. As noted earlier, to navigate this new era of AI synergy, we must attend not to distant futures but to the *ethical horizon*—the edge where today transitions into tomorrow.

The ethical horizon does not predict the future but actively creates it, empowering us to take meaningful action in the present moment. Just as a geographical horizon marks the visible limit of our immediate perception, our ethical horizon represents the boundary where current understanding meets tomorrow's unfolding possibilities. This framing empowers libraries to exercise agency while maintaining clarity about *who we are* and *who we are becoming*.

> Our ethical horizon is not a distant boundary but a liminal edge where present actions shape emerging potential.

The ethical horizon concept is particularly relevant to libraries preparing for AI integration. It transforms abstract discussions into concrete questions about immediate actions and their consequences. Standing at this horizon, libraries exercise agency by:

- Crafting today's decisions as seeds of tomorrow's possibilities
- Transforming AI literacy from technical skill to collective imagination
- Turning each strategic choice into a bridge between current capabilities and emerging potential
- Practicing advocacy as an act of collective technological dreaming

This orientation empowers libraries to move beyond reactive resistance or passive acceptance and claim active agency in shaping how AI develops and impacts our communities. The ethical horizon reminds us that while we cannot perfectly predict the future, we can intentionally shape it through our choices, actions, and advocacy today.

IMAGINATION: THE FORCE THAT SHAPES OUR ETHICAL HORIZON

Engagement at the ethical horizon requires more than recognition of our agency; it demands imagination. Like an invisible force of gravity determining the movement of celestial bodies, imagination is the essential catalyst that draws us toward new possibilities while keeping us oriented to our core values. It both provides the creative energy to envision AI integration and is the magnetic pull guiding our direction.

Imagination serves as a transformative force in three crucial ways. First, it is a catalyst for action. When we imagine new possibilities for human–AI synergy, we move beyond both paralyzing anxiety and uncritical acceptance. Imagination empowers us to envision specific ways AI can enhance rather than diminish human capabilities, transforming abstract potential into concrete initiatives. Second, it is a compass for ethical development. Imagination helps us navigate between what is technically possible and what is ethically desirable. It enables us to envision futures where AI serves human and ecological flourishing, directing our immediate decisions and actions. Third, it is a bridge between resistance and innovation. Thoughtful imagination helps us see beyond constraints while remaining grounded in our fundamental values and commitments.

This creative tension between imagination and ethical consideration guides decision-making. As imaginative mediators, libraries can

- Craft AI services that amplify human connections.
- Transform AI literacy into collective empowerment.
- Design ethical frameworks that protect human dignity.
- Create collaborative spaces where technology builds community.

Imagination is a generative, transformative force that recognizes and shapes potential synergies, supplying the ends toward which *protopian thinking* informs the means of AI integration.[4] The concept of "protopia" offers an alternative to the nightmarish dysfunctionality of dystopia and the unrealistic paradise of utopia. The term "protopia" envisions progress that is incremental day by day or over a longer period of time, rather than revolutionary or perfect: It involves steady, thoughtful steps toward a better future, where each improvement brings new benefits and challenges. Protopian thinking acknowledges that progress is complex and requires constant attention to ensure that it serves the flourishing of all. Protopian thinking transforms imagination into a compass guiding libraries toward a future that we incrementally, intentionally, and carefully create.

> Where limited imagination can fuel resistance to AI, expansive imagination opens pathways to thoughtful integration.

CORE VALUES: ORIENTING FORCES IN OUR GRAVITATIONAL SYSTEM

As libraries navigate AI integration, five core values serve as orienting forces, creating a matrix through which imagination flows and ethical action emerges. These core values are transparency, curiosity, rigor, inclusion, and play. Like the fundamental forces that shape celestial motion, these values create dynamic fields of influence—guiding, generating, and transforming how libraries engage with technological potential.

Transparency

Transparency encompasses the clarity of our systems and the openness of our practices. For AI tools, it's the extent to which a platform clarifies its methodologies, algorithms, and data sources for users. It also involves how users share their work; a transparent AI tool enables students to share findings, processes, and conversation threads with instructors. In this way, transparency enhances trust, reducing suspicions of dishonesty and promoting openness. *Transparency illuminates*. This value establishes the context of trust in which *curiosity* can flourish.

Curiosity

Curiosity reflects a commitment to exploring new possibilities while maintaining our critical grounding. This value motivates desire-driven discovery; it moves us to ask questions, seek unexpected connections, and imagine new applications of AI in service to our communities. When applied to AI tools, curiosity reflects how a tool generates surprising insights, uncovers connections that prompt further investigation, and inspires users to explore new ideas. This value fosters a spirit of discovery and innovation. *Curiosity disrupts* our normal expectations in a dynamic activity that is helpfully constrained by *rigor*.

Rigor

We purposefully reclaim rigor from narrow definitions focused on productivity metrics and inflexible standards. In our framework, rigor means the thoughtful application of accuracy, reliability, and scholarly validity in ways that enhance rather than diminish human capability. This re-conceptualization of rigor emphasizes a commitment to excellence while maintaining flexibility, creativity, and responsiveness to human needs. It ensures that AI tools meet academic standards and can be confidently used in research and scholarly work. *Rigor interrogates*. This value balances high standards with accessibility, maintaining excellence while prioritizing *inclusion*.

Inclusion

Inclusion ensures that AI integration serves all members of our communities equitably and respectfully. This means considering diverse needs, abilities, perspectives, and access requirements in every aspect of AI implementation. Inclusion extends beyond mere accessibility to embrace representation in AI development, cultural sensitivity in implementation, and the equitable distribution of benefits. Libraries must actively work to identify and address barriers to AI access and understanding, and thus ensure that AI integration doesn't exacerbate existing inequities but helps bridge them instead. *Inclusion reimagines*, ensuring that tools serve and represent diverse human experiences and also maintain welcoming spaces for *play*.

Play

Play creates space for creativity and learning through engagement. By encouraging a playful exploration of AI tools and concepts, libraries can help reduce anxiety around new technologies. Play enables safe experimentation with AI capabilities and recognizes the importance of user experience in learning and exploration. An AI tool that embodies the value of play is one that users find motivating and enjoyable. The joy and satisfaction derived from these interactions, including the enjoyment experienced through conversing with AI, are central to this value and enhance learning and creativity. *Play improvises.* Play does not diminish the seriousness of our purpose but instead provides an engaging path toward meaningful learning and innovation.

The five core values here are not isolated principles but gravitational forces that continuously shape and reshape each other. Transparency enables curiosity, curiosity demands rigor, rigor supports inclusion, and inclusion creates space for play. They interact continuously, generating fields of influence that guide decision-making, service design, and community engagement. They create a dynamic matrix that shapes how libraries approach AI integration. This matrix helps us evaluate potential AI implementations, design new services, and measure success in ways that align with our human-centered approach. Core values ensure that as we move toward our ethical horizon, we do so in ways that promote the flourishing of all participants in our information ecosystem.

DISCERNING VALUES IN TOOLS

Our core values provide a matrix for imagining services that are charged with their essential energies:

Transparency. Imagine a library recommendation system that *illuminates* the intellectual cartography between texts, revealing unexpected connections. This system doesn't just suggest books but visually maps connections, showing users the intricate web of knowledge underlying each recommendation. Patrons trace how an algorithm discovered unexpected links, thus transforming passive consumption into active intellectual exploration.

Curiosity. A research librarian uses AI to analyze historical archives, uncovering new insights that were previously unrecognizable. The tool doesn't replace human insight but creates a collaborative dialogue between technological pattern recognition and human interpretive skill, revealing historical narratives that no single researcher could have imagined. The tool *disrupts* assumptions, creating collaborative dialogues that challenge established frameworks.

Rigor. Think of an AI-powered tool that facilitates "conversations" with long-dead philosophers and thought leaders. It learns from diverse writing styles, adapting to convey individual voices while maintaining scholarly integrity. The tool exemplifies adaptive learning and functions as a generative hermeneutic device. It *interrogates* epistemic diversity by creating nuanced dialogues that reveal how different philosophical traditions understand knowledge, communication, and human experience across time.

Inclusion. Imagine a multilingual AI translation service that captures cultural nuances and contextual meaning. It learns from community input, continuously expanding its understanding to represent marginalized linguistic experiences. It thus turns translation from a technical task into an act of cultural preservation and respect. AI-empowered translation *reimagines* linguistic representation, continuously expanding our understanding beyond traditional communicative boundaries.

Play. Think of a library workshop that *improvises* creative possibilities, blending machine learning with human emotional intelligence to explore technological potential. In this workshop, patrons collaboratively design AI-human creative projects, perhaps generating poetry that blends machine learning with human emotional intelligence. Participants explore AI's creative potential as a playful extension of human imagination, reducing technological anxiety through shared exploration.

ORIENTING QUESTIONS: EVALUATING AI'S IMPACT ON HUMAN *BEING*

As noted earlier, while we navigate AI integration guided by our core values, two fundamental questions serve as an essential rubric for evaluation and decision-making: What does AI do *to* human *being* in the world? What does AI do *for* human *being* in the world? These simple questions provide a meaningful framework for examining AI's impact while keeping human and ecological flourishing at the center. Like complementary forces in our gravitational system, they work in tension to create balanced, thoughtful approaches to AI integration.

Agency in Questioning: From Evaluation to Action

These orienting questions are more than analytical tools—they express our gravitational agency across personal, institutional, and ecosystem levels. When we ask what AI does to and for human *being*, we aren't passive observers of technological change but active shapers of how it unfolds in our communities.

At the personal level, these questions guide individual librarians in exercising discernment and ethical judgment. They help us evaluate specific AI tools, decide how to integrate them into our workflows and institutional practice, and determine how to guide patrons in their use. A reference librarian asking what a new AI search tool does to and for human research capabilities is exercising personal agency—making choices that will shape how that technology influences their community's information landscape.

At the institutional level, these questions inform collective decisions about AI adoption, policy development, and service design. When a library committee systematically examines what a potential AI implementation might do to and for their community, they exercise institutional agency—creating gravitational influence that extends throughout their organization and beyond. This questioning becomes the basis for thoughtful policies that guide responsible AI integration and serve as models for others.

At the ecosystem level, these questions become frameworks for collective advocacy and collaborative action. When library associations ask what emerging AI developments do to and for human *being* in the world, they mobilize collective agency to engage the developers of these tools, influence policy, develop shared standards, and shape public discourse. Through such questioning, the library ecosystem exerts its gravitational pull on broader societal conversations about technology and humanity.

These orienting questions transform understanding into action in each sphere. They remind us that our role is not simply to seek to understand generative AI's impact but to actively shape it through intentional choices and advocacy. By moving from questioning to action, we manifest our agency as individuals and communities, ensuring that AI integration advances rather than diminishes human capability and flourishing.

What does AI do *to* human *being* in the world?

This first question prompts us to critically examine the potential negative impacts of AI development and integration on people and communities. It encourages us to problematize AI's effects, considering issues such as exacerbating inequities, environmental impacts, job displacement, misinformation and disinformation, privacy or pedagogical concerns, and so on. AI contributes to these challenges, but AI is not the sole cause. These challenges are perennial and pervasive human concerns that predate AI. As stewards of (in)formation in an increasingly AI-powered society, librarians are responsible for addressing these issues in the context of AI integration.

While we must consider AI's environmental footprint and other potential harms, these considerations should be placed in the broader context of our global systems and practices. Rather than treating generative AI as uniquely problematic, libraries can model thoughtful integration that acknowledges these concerns while recognizing that most of the challenges that generative AI presents aren't new but are extensions of long-standing human concerns. Our role as stewards of (in)formation positions us to address these issues with nuance and perspective, avoiding both uncritical acceptance and disproportionate anxiety about AI's impacts.

We can then problematize AI's effects through the lens of our core values. *Transparency*, for example, demands that we clarify the hidden biases in AI systems and reveal the environmental impacts from AI infrastructure and energy use. *Rigor* requires us to carefully evaluate AI's effects on work and professional identity, its impacts on learning and cognitive development, and its consequences for information access and literacy gaps. Again, we recognize that many challenges AI presents aren't new but extensions of perennial human concerns. Libraries' role as centers of gravity positions us to address these impacts thoughtfully and proactively.

What does AI do *for* human *being* in the world?

The second question invites us to imagine and cultivate AI's potential benefits for human flourishing. Our values guide us toward generative possibilities: *Curiosity* encourages us to explore how AI might enhance human creativity and problem-solving, enable new forms of discovery and learning, and foster encounters across cultural differences. *Inclusion* ensures that we consider AI's potential to increase accessibility, bridge existing digital and information divides, and support diverse learning styles, needs, and abilities. *Play* helps us envision ways AI could create new spaces for collaboration and innovation, support personal and professional growth, and enable more engaging forms of learning and discovery.

Our fundamental questions prompt new synergies as partnerships between human and AI minds are forged to overcome challenges and actualize potential, turning questions into action.

FROM QUESTIONS TO ACTION

These orienting frames and questions transform abstract ethical considerations into practical tools for decision-making. When evaluating any AI implementation, libraries should:

- Examine both its potential benefits and harms systematically.
- Consider its impacts across diverse communities and contexts.
- Evaluate its alignment with core values and ethical commitments.
- Identify the opportunities for enhancing human capabilities.
- Plan for monitoring and adjusting based on observed impacts.

Our position as centers of gravity in the information ecosystem makes the questions of what AI does to and for human *being* in the world particularly crucial. We ask these questions as part of our broader obligation to shape AI integration in ways that serve the common good. Through careful questioning, we exercise our agency in building toward the futures that we envision, ensuring that AI development enhances rather than diminishes human capability and community well-being.

THE TRANSFORMING LIBRARY ECOSYSTEM: BECOMING CENTERS OF GRAVITY

As libraries strengthen their position as centers of gravity for AI integration, transformation occurs not through revolutionary change but through a thoughtful evolution of our fundamental roles and capabilities. This evolution manifests in different ways across the library ecosystem, yet it remains grounded in our core values and commitment to human flourishing. Different types of libraries are transforming to serve as centers of gravity in ways that reflect their unique communities and missions.

Public libraries evolve as community hubs where AI literacy becomes part of digital citizenship. They create gravitational fields that:

- Draw diverse community members into conversations about AI
- Support equitable access to AI tools and learning
- Ground technological advances in community needs and workforce empowerment
- Balance innovation with inclusion and accessibility

Academic libraries transform into laboratories for ethical AI integration in research and learning. Their gravitational influence:

- Shapes campus conversations about AI and academic integrity
- Guides faculty and students in responsible AI use
- Connects theoretical frameworks with practical applications
- Supports innovative research while upholding ethical standards

School libraries become spaces where young learners develop a foundational understanding of AI. They create fields that:

- Foster critical thinking about technology
- Support teachers in thoughtful AI integration
- Help students develop healthy relationships with AI tools
- Build foundations for lifelong technological literacy

Special libraries evolve as specialized centers for AI implementation in professional contexts. Their influence:

- Guides domain-specific AI applications
- Ensures ethical use in specialized fields
- Connects professional practice with technological innovation
- Maintains human expertise while leveraging AI capabilities

Maintaining Balance Through Transformation

As libraries transform, they maintain equilibrium between stability and change by grounding new services in enduring values, evolving existing roles rather than replacing them, building on established trust while embracing innovation, and strengthening human connections through technological change. This balanced transformation positions libraries to guide their communities toward thoughtful AI integration while maintaining their essential character as centers of human learning and connection, public trust, and centers of gravity in an AI-literate society. It prepares us for the practical implementation considerations we'll explore in the next section.

CONCLUSION: CLAIMING AGENCY, BUILDING FUTURES

As we stand at our ethical horizon—where today meets tomorrow—libraries' position as centers of gravity in the AI landscape becomes both opportunity and obligation. This positioning isn't merely metaphorical; it represents our fundamental agency in shaping how AI develops and impacts our world. Through our gravitational influence, we create fields where human values orient technological progress, imagination catalyzes positive change, and thoughtful evolution overcomes uncritical adoption.

This evolution manifests throughout the library ecosystem. In each context, libraries function as centers of gravity: primary sources of stability, critical points of influence, and cores around which other elements productively revolve. Though this influence, like gravity itself, may often go unnoticed, it remains essential to the functioning of our information ecosystem.

A human-centered paradigm for AI in libraries isn't about asserting human supremacy over technology. Instead, it recognizes our responsibility to exercise agency in the service of human and ecological flourishing. By claiming this agency—through core values, orienting questions, and transforming practices—we actively shape AI integration in ways that enhance rather than diminish human *being* and *doing*.

As we move forward to consider practical implementation, we carry with us these essential understandings:

- Our position *between* and *below* creates both opportunity and obligation.
- Our values orient us toward ethical horizons.
- Our questions guide thoughtful action.
- Our transformation strengthens our gravitational influence.
- Our agency empowers us to build the futures we envision.

Thus, the human-centered paradigm becomes a philosophical framework and a practical approach to claiming our role in an AI-enhanced world. Through it, libraries maintain their essential character while evolving to meet new challenges, always oriented toward the flourishing of the communities and world we serve.

NOTES

1. See the discussion of "betweenness" in various chapters of Bret W. Davis, ed., *The Oxford Handbook of Japanese Philosophy* (Oxford: Oxford University Press, 2020).
2. For an insightful and compelling consideration of human agency as the dynamo that shapes the development and trajectories of technology, see Verity Harding, *AI Needs You: How We Can Change AI's Future and Save Our Own* (Princeton, NJ: Princeton University Press, 2024).
3. For a groundbreaking examination of the ethical, ecological, and human costs of AI development—concerns that remain critical despite the field's rapid evolution—see Kate Crawford, *Atlas of AI: Power, Politics, and the Planetary Costs of Artificial Intelligence* (New Haven, CT: Yale University Press, 2021).
4. The futurist Kevin Kelly coined the term "protopia" to describe a third orientation to the future that envisions neither utopia nor dystopia but rather one that looks for incremental or "subtle" progress day by day. See Kevin Kelly, *The Inevitable: Understanding the 12 Technological Forces That Will Shape Our Future* (New York: Viking, 2016).

3

Essential Concepts and Definitions

Imagination is the energy by which libraries transform abstract potential into concrete capability. So far we have imagined libraries as crucial centers of gravity in an AI-literate society, a metaphor both poetic and practical. Where chapter 2 established our philosophical positioning as centers of gravity in the Age of Intelligence, this chapter provides a basic, essential grammar and conceptual infrastructure within which libraries exert their gravitational pull. Admittedly, this chapter may feel like a stone skipping across the surface of deeper waters; our aim is to provide a basic introduction to AI-related technologies and issues in libraries, and we point to several resources to guide further exploration. This chapter moves from technical description to philosophical exploration, ultimately positioning libraries as dynamic spaces of human–AI collaboration. This chapter progresses through five sections:

1. *But First, Imagination (Again)*. We return to our discussion of imagination as a crucial force.
2. *Key AI Technologies for Libraries: A Practical Orientation*. We introduce key AI technologies (large language models, machine learning, etc.) that have practical library applications.
3. *Defining AI in Library Contexts: The Power of Synergy*. We explore *synergy* with a collaborative co-intelligence.
4. *Prophets, Priests, and Curators: Navigating Imagination in AI Integration*. We look to "prophets and priests" as a guiding metaphor for navigating the inevitable tensions in technological change.

5. *Metaliteracy: Expanding the Imaginative Landscape.* We describe how metaliteracy offers a multifaceted, integrative approach to AI literacy.

By defining essential terms, unpacking key technologies, and situating AI literacy within our existing ecosystem of multiliteracies, we lay the groundwork for libraries to become pivotal architects of AI integration as we build toward the futures we imagine.

BUT FIRST, IMAGINATION (AGAIN)

Chapter 2 described imagination as the critical mediating force between technological potential and human agency. When expansive, imagination enables us to envision AI as a collaborative partner rather than a threatening replacement. It helps us explore innovative ways that AI can augment human capabilities, create ethical frameworks that center human dignity, and bridge technological possibilities with human-centered values. Conversely, a failure of imagination often accompanies fear-based responses to technological change or defensive positioning against AI integration. While our suspicion of AI and our acknowledgment of its potential pitfalls do not indicate a lack of imagination (on the contrary, these are necessary perspectives), uncritical fear, abject dismissal, or a refusal to engage will result in missed opportunities for meaningful human–AI synergy and a reductive understanding of AI's potential to enhance the public good.

Imagination becomes the magnetic force that orients AI competencies toward human flourishing, preventing them from becoming detached or potentially harmful. In libraries, cultivating imagination means creating spaces for curiosity, play, and reflective exploration. It's about helping our communities see AI not as a threat but as a new technology shaped by human intention and ethical commitment that finds application in new and emerging tools. Imagination is more than a cognitive skill; it is a profound ethical practice that maintains human agency in technological transformation.

This imaginative orientation allows us to approach the essential grammar of AI technologies not as abstract technical concepts but as tools that can be shaped and directed toward human flourishing. By understanding these foundational elements through the lens of imagination, we can better envision how they might serve our communities and advance our mission.

To transform this imaginative potential into practical capability, we must first become familiar with the key AI technologies that are reshaping the information landscape. As with any new language, learning the essential grammar of AI enables more nuanced expression and understanding. We'll explore each technology's technical foundations and potential human-centered applications in library contexts, emphasizing how it can enhance rather than replace human capabilities.

KEY AI TECHNOLOGIES FOR LIBRARIES: A PRACTICAL ORIENTATION

Librarians don't need to become technical experts in artificial intelligence, but we must develop a nuanced understanding that enables thoughtful integration and critical evaluation of this new technology. We aim to demystify these concepts, providing librarians with sufficient conceptual clarity to make informed decisions about AI implementation.[1]

Large Language Models

Technical description: Large language models (LLMs) are advanced AI models trained on massive text corpora using deep learning techniques capable of understanding and generating human-like text and other modalities.[2]

Like an infinitely expansive library catalog that can generate, interpret, and respond to complex queries, LLMs represent a powerful tool for extending human capabilities. We should imagine LLMs not as a replacement for the reference librarian but as a collaborative partnership where human expertise is augmented by AI's ability to process vast amounts of text and other data.

In libraries, LLMs enable human-centered applications, like:

- Enhanced reference services that preserve librarian expertise while expanding reach
- Personalized learning support that adapts to individual needs
- Multilingual communication that breaks down language barriers
- Accessibility services that make information more available to diverse users

This technology also raises ethical considerations,[3] such as:

- Maintaining transparency about AI involvement in services
- Ensuring equitable access while acknowledging limitations

- Preserving human judgment in critical decision-making
- Protecting patron privacy and data security

Through imaginative implementation, LLMs can become catalysts for deeper human connections, more inclusive services, enhanced learning experiences, and expanded access to knowledge.

Machine Learning

Technical description: Machine learning is a computational approach that enables systems to improve their performance through experience without explicit programming.[4]

Like a librarian who becomes increasingly skilled at recommendations through patron interactions, machine learning helps systems recognize patterns and make increasingly accurate decisions. In libraries, this human-centered capability enables enhanced search experiences, personalized recommendations, and predictive collection management—all while preserving and centering librarian expertise as the guiding force behind these services.

Natural Language Processing

Technical description: Natural language processing is a computational linguistics field that is focused on enabling computers to understand, interpret, and generate human language.[5]

Like a multilingual reference librarian who can translate complex queries and communicate across linguistic contexts, natural language processing helps computers comprehend and process human language. In libraries, this enables intelligent chatbots for patron support, automated summarization, multilingual assistance, and enhanced accessibility services while maintaining a human touch.

Generative Artificial Intelligence

Technical description: Generative AI (or GenAI) refers to AI systems that create new content such as text, images, audio, and video by recognizing patterns in data they were trained on. These systems use neural networks to transform user inputs into new outputs by predicting what should come next in a sequence. GenAI tools can generate original content, modify existing work, or assist with creative and technical tasks based on the instructions they receive.[6]

As we mentioned before, generative AI is an *arrival technology*. Like electricity and the printing press, whether we opt in or out, this technology will become ubiquitous and will transform learning and work. Think of generative AI not as a replacement for human creativity, but as a collaborative research assistant who can help brainstorm ideas, draft summaries, and suggest unexpected connections. This technology extends human creative and analytical capabilities while nevertheless raising important questions about authenticity, originality, and the nature of creation itself.

For libraries, human-centered applications for GenAI abound and include:

- Research support that sparks new insights while preserving academic integrity
- Metadata creation that enhances discoverability while maintaining quality
- Accessibility improvements that expand access while respecting user needs
- Educational content development that enriches learning while supporting pedagogy
- Discovery tools that inspire exploration while guiding thoughtful use

In libraries, GenAI also requires ethical considerations, like:

- Maintaining transparency about AI-generated content
- Protecting intellectual property and attribution
- Ensuring equitable access to creative tools
- Supporting responsible use in academic contexts
- Preserving human agency in creative processes

Neural Networks

Technical description: Neural networks are computational systems modeled after the neural connections in the human brain and are designed to recognize complex patterns.[7]

Similar to how experienced librarians can quickly identify nuanced connections between seemingly unrelated resources, neural networks process information through interconnected nodes. This enables advanced search algorithms, collection analysis, and research trend mapping, enhancing rather than replacing human expertise.

Algorithmic Systems

Technical description: Algorithmic systems are structured sets of step-by-step instructions for solving computational problems.

Like a meticulously designed library classification system, algorithms provide clear, repeatable processes for achieving specific outcomes. An algorithm is simply a step-by-step recipe for solving problems. Just as a cookie recipe guides bakers from ingredients to a delicious treat, algorithms guide computers through complex tasks—sorting library inventory or recommending the perfect book, for example.

In libraries, algorithms can facilitate human-centered applications, like:

- Collection organization that reflects community needs
- Resource allocation that promotes equity
- User experience optimization that preserves human agency
- Research workflows that enhance discovery

But they also require ethical considerations,[8] such as:

- Transparency in decision-making processes
- Bias awareness and mitigation
- Fair and equitable resource distribution
- Privacy protection in automated systems

Understanding these various technologies is more than a technical exercise. Each one represents a potential partnership, a way of extending librarian capabilities beyond traditional boundaries. Synergy emerges not from the technologies themselves, but from how we imagine and implement them in the service of human knowledge and connection. This transformative process requires us to think deeply about how AI and human intelligence can work together in library contexts, moving beyond simple automation to true collaboration.

> As libraries exert their gravitational influence, AI technologies become more than isolated tools—they become part of a dynamic ecosystem where human imagination shapes technological potential.

DEFINING AI IN LIBRARY CONTEXTS: THE POWER OF SYNERGY

The word "synergy" derives from the Greek term "synergos," meaning "working together"—a profound etymology that captures the essence of human-AI collaboration. In libraries, synergy represents not a technological takeover but a nuanced partnership where human expertise and artificial intelligence combine to create capabilities greater than either one could achieve independently. Collaborative co-intelligence emerges as a transformative approach to AI integration.[9] This concept positions AI as a tool for augmentation, not replacement—a partner that enhances human capabilities rather than supplanting them.

This means reimagining library services as dynamic ecosystems where AI serves as a sophisticated assistant. A reference librarian using AI might quickly generate comprehensive research overviews, freeing up time to provide more focused, personalized guidance. A cataloger could leverage AI to streamline metadata creation, focusing human expertise on complex classification challenges that require nuanced judgment. A collection development specialist might use AI to identify emerging research trends but would ultimately rely on human insight to make strategic acquisition decisions.

> GenAI amplifies librarian capabilities by extending reach, enhancing precision, and creating space for more meaningful, creative work.

The collaborative model fundamentally respects human agency. This approach aligns with libraries' enduring mission: connecting people with knowledge in ways that are thoughtful, ethical, and profoundly human. If synergy represents the "how" of human-AI collaboration, then imagination represents the "why"—the generative force that transforms technological tools into meaningful partnerships.

Collaborative Co-Intelligence: Imagination in Action

Imagination is the essential catalyst that transforms AI from a technological tool to a dynamic partner in human creativity and problem-solving. Just as chapter 2 positioned imagination as the invisible gravitational force that shapes our ethical horizon, we see imagination as the generative energy that enables true synergy between human and artificial intelligence. Collaborative co-intelligence is not about replacement but about creative amplification. Imagination empowers this co-creation by:

- Bridging computational capabilities with human creativity
- Generating unexpected connections and insights
- Expanding the boundaries of what's possible through collaborative thinking
- Transforming AI from a passive tool to an active creative partner

Imagination aligns technological potential with human intentionality, allowing us to see AI as a collaborative intelligence that can extend our creative and analytical capacities. Imagination does not exist in a vacuum. It manifests through diverse perspectives, tensions, and collaborative approaches. The metaphor of "prophets and priests" reveals the dynamic landscape where imagination takes shape.

PROPHETS, PRIESTS, AND CURATORS: NAVIGATING IMAGINATION IN AI INTEGRATION

Imagination in AI integration is not about uncritical techno-optimism but about creating space for multiple perspectives. The metaphor of "prophets and priests" offers a meaningful framework for understanding librarians' diverse responses to technological change.

Prophets are those who push for innovation, explore AI's transformative potential, and imagine new possibilities for library services. *Priests* are those who maintain institutional memory, protect core values, and ensure careful, measured technological integration.

Critically, both roles are essential. Resistance and suspicion are not weaknesses but rather reflect necessary strengths. Nevertheless, all librarians must develop AI literacy, regardless of their place on the prophet-priest spectrum. Resistance must be an informed resistance. Those who will meaningfully participate in resistance must also be AI-literate. *Everyone must level up.*

Curators emerge as a critical third perspective—librarians who carefully select and critically evaluate AI tools. Curators understand AI's limitations and potential pitfalls, and they can consciously decide when and how to incorporate technologies while maintaining human expertise and judgment. Imagination becomes the gravitational force that holds these different perspectives in productive orbit, creating a space where prophetic innovation and priestly caution coexist and complement each other.

This approach validates different perspectives while emphasizing the necessity of AI literacy. It recognizes that imagination is not about blind acceptance but creating meaningful dialogue and thoughtful, inclusive integration. If prophets and priests represent different approaches to technological adaptation, *metaliteracy* provides the conceptual framework that allows these approaches to coexist and evolve.

METALITERACY: EXPANDING THE IMAGINATIVE LANDSCAPE

Imagination is the gravitational force enabling movement between technological potential and human values; metaliteracy provides the conceptual infrastructure that gives shape and structure to this gravitational field. Just as the "prophets and priests" metaphor revealed the dynamic tension inherent in technological adaptation, metaliteracy offers a framework for understanding how we navigate and make sense of complex information ecosystems.

What Is Metaliteracy?

Metaliteracy reimagines information literacy for today's digital world. As defined by Mackey and Jacobson, metaliteracy is a comprehensive framework that empowers individuals to critically evaluate, create, share, and reflect on information in collaborative digital environments.[10] Think of it as expanding traditional information literacy (finding and evaluating information) to include creating, sharing, and reflecting on information across digital spaces. It emphasizes that learners aren't just consumers of information—they're active participants who need to understand how to navigate and contribute to our connected world. The key difference is that while traditional information literacy focuses on finding and evaluating sources, metaliteracy adds crucial skills like:

- Understanding how social media shapes information
- Creating and sharing digital content responsibly
- Adapting to new technologies
- Reflecting on one's own learning and sharing practices

Metaliteracy operates across four essential learning domains—cognitive, metacognitive, behavioral, and affective—recognizing that effective engagement with information environments requires intellectual understanding, reflective awareness, practical skills, and appropriate attitudes. These four domains provide a holistic approach to learning that is particularly relevant for libraries approaching AI literacy.

While information literacy helps users evaluate information found through search tools, metaliteracy prepares users for active participation in dynamic information environments where they both consume and create—precisely the relationship users have with generative AI tools. In fact, we propose that metaliteracy is AI literacy, as both concern themselves fundamentally with critical evaluation, collaborative creation, and ethical engagement with information in digital spaces.

> Metaliteracy involves and incorporates all of the literacies that are the core of library instruction. It represents a transformative approach to understanding literacy in complex, interconnected information ecosystems.

This connection becomes particularly evident when we consider that collaborative co-creation with generative AI tools directly mirrors the active, reflective information production that metaliteracy addresses. When a user crafts prompts for an AI system, evaluates the generated content, refines their approach, and produces new knowledge through this iterative process, they are engaging in all four domains of metaliteracy simultaneously: The cognitive understanding of AI capabilities, metacognitive reflection on the interaction process, behavioral strategies for effective prompting, and affective responses to the collaborative experience all play crucial roles in effective AI use.

By positioning AI literacy as an expression of metaliteracy, libraries can build upon established instructional approaches rather than developing entirely new frameworks. This approach acknowledges that the fundamental skills needed for thoughtful AI engagement are extensions of the skills that libraries have cultivated for years. In chapter 7, we'll explore more deeply how metaliteracy provides the foundation for our gravitational model of AI literacy and informs our seven frames for instruction.

Four Domains of Metaliteracy

Metaliteracy involves four domains—affective, behavioral, cognitive, and metacognitive. These domains align well with our conviction that AI literacy is metaliteracy:

1. *Cognitive domain (thinking)*. This domain emphasizes understanding AI technologies and analyzing their epistemological and techno-social implications. The cognitive domain is about:

   » Comprehending AI technologies and their underlying mechanisms
   » Developing a critical understanding of AI capabilities and limitations
   » Analyzing the information generated by AI systems
   » Constructing knowledge through complex technological interactions

   The cognitive domain focuses on understanding AI concepts, the critical evaluation of AI outputs, and comprehension of how AI systems work. This includes recognizing AI biases, understanding the difference between various AI tools, and knowing when (and when not) to use AI.

2. *Metacognitive domain (thinking about thinking)*. This domain encourages learners to monitor their thinking and to integrate new learning when working with AI. They do this by:

   » Reflecting on their learning and engagement with AI technologies
   » Monitoring their personal understanding and strategic approach to AI tools
   » Developing their self-awareness about technological mediation
   » Evaluating their personal learning strategies in AI-enhanced environments

   The metacognitive domain involves reflecting on one's own learning and thinking processes while using AI. This includes monitoring one's AI usage patterns, adapting strategies based on outcomes, and continuously evaluating one's approach to AI integration.

3. *Behavioral domain (doing).* This domain considers skills, competencies, and adaptive strategies developed through AI use and engagement. Learners act in this domain by:

    » Practicing ethical and strategic engagement with AI technologies
    » Developing practical skills for responsible AI interaction
    » Creating adaptive workflows that integrate human and machine capabilities
    » Demonstrating technical proficiency and discernment

    The behavioral domain encompasses the practical skills and actions in using AI effectively. This includes learning prompt engineering, understanding AI capabilities and limitations, and developing responsible AI usage habits.

4. *Affective domain (feeling).* This domain involves our emotional responses and attitudes toward learning with AI. Growth in this domain includes:

    » Cultivating emotional intelligence in technological interactions
    » Managing technological anxiety and uncertainty
    » Developing curiosity and openness to technological innovation
    » Maintaining human agency and emotional resilience

    The affective domain involves managing emotions and attitudes while engaging with AI tools. This includes developing confidence in AI interactions, maintaining healthy skepticism, and managing anxiety about AI's impact on work and society.

The four domains provide a robust framework for developing AI literacy. The cognitive domain understands AI technologies; the metacognitive domain reflects on engagement; the behavioral domain practices creative and ethical interaction; and the affective domain manages emotions and agency. Since it involves the multiliteracies that are the core of our instruction, metaliteracy positions libraries as translational spaces for bridging technological understanding with durable skills and core values.

Especially in our use of generative AI, metaliteracy helps us reimagine knowledge production as a dynamic, collaborative process where humans and AI co-create understanding rather than viewing AI as a passive tool. Given this observation (AI as a co-creator of knowledge and understanding), our conceptualization of metaliteracy will likely expand. At the very least, we'll need to create new methodologies for evaluating the credibility of AI-generated content and establish new protocols for attributing collaborative knowledge creation. In the meantime, metaliteracy helps us recognize AI literacy as a holistic, adaptive approach to technological engagement that maintains human agency and critical thinking.

AI LITERACY AS METALITERACY IN PRACTICE

AI literacy is a dynamic, multi-dimensional practice that emerges from the interplay of metaliteracy's four domains. In other words, AI literacy is not a discrete skill but a complex, adaptive practice that emerges from the interplay of these domains. It exists within a broader ecosystem of multiliteracies, drawing from and contributing to information, digital, media, and technological literacies. By understanding AI literacy through the metaliteracy framework, we recognize it as:

- A dynamic, evolving competency
- An integrated approach to technological engagement
- A practice of continuous learning and adaptation
- A way of maintaining human agency in technological transformation

Metaliteracy, like imagination, transcends boundaries; it represents a multidimensional approach to understanding and navigating complex information landscapes. The four domains of metaliteracy map to the imaginative and adaptive approach we've been discussing:

1. *Cognitive domain*: This domain resonates with the "prophetic" impulse of understanding and exploring new technological possibilities.
2. *Metacognitive domain*: This domain reflects the "priestly" practice of critical reflection and institutional memory.
3. *Behavioral domain*: This domain represents the "curator's" practical, strategic approach to technology integration.
4. *Affective domain*: This domain captures the emotional and creative energy of imagination itself.

Metaliteracy is a mode of imaginative engagement that allows us to move fluidly between technological potential and human values. It provides the conceptual infrastructure that enables libraries to exert their gravitational pull, transforming abstract technological potential into concrete, human-centered capabilities. (Chapter 7 explores metaliteracy as the mode and medium for AI literacy.)

CONCLUSION: GRAVITATIONAL PULL AND IMAGINATIVE POTENTIAL

As we navigate the complex landscape of AI integration, libraries' gravitational influence becomes ever more critical, creating dynamic spaces where technological potential and human values are held in productive tension. This chapter has mapped a basic conceptual terrain, revealing AI as a collaborative intelligence that can be shaped by imagination, ethical commitment, and strategic insight. Metaliteracy provides the conceptual infrastructure to move fluidly between technological possibility and human intention. We explore a middle way between a wholesale embrace and a reflexive rejection of AI integration. This moment requires thoughtful, adaptive approaches to this new kind of technological integration.

AI integration is about cultivating:

- Curiosity over certainty
- Adaptability over rigidity
- Collaborative intelligence over isolated expertise
- Ethical imagination over technological determinism

As we progress, libraries will more profoundly emerge as generative spaces where human creativity and technological capability co-create new forms of knowledge, understanding, and connection. Chapter 4 explores practical strategies for implementing this vision, transforming these conceptual insights into tangible pathways for AI integration.

NOTES

1. The glossary we offer in this chapter is by no means comprehensive and intends to provide a basic familiarity with key AI concepts and their application in library contexts. For fuller discussion and more comprehensive coverage of AI-related terms, see Richard R. Khan, *The AI Glossary: Demystifying 101 Essential Artificial Intelligence Terms for Everyone* (Boca Raton, FL: CRC, 2025).
2. IBM, "What Are LLMs?" November 2, 2023, www.ibm.com/think/topics/large-language-models.
3. As previously discussed, the ethics of AI feels like a moving target since the field is developing so rapidly. However, for an anchor to AI and ethics that seems relevant despite the shifting landscape, see Markus D. Dubber, Frank Pasquale, and Sunit Das, eds., *The Oxford Handbook of Ethics of AI* (New York: Oxford University Press, 2020).
4. ISO, "Machine Learning (ML): All There Is to Know," www.iso.org/artificial-intelligence/machine-learning.
5. AWS, "What Is Natural Language Processing (NLP)?" https://aws.amazon.com/what-is/nlp/.
6. Nvidia, "What Is Generative AI?" www.nvidia.com/en-us/glossary/generative-ai/.
7. AWS, "What Is a Neural Network?" https://aws.amazon.com/what-is/neural-network/.
8. Here, we merely point to ethical concerns that others profoundly address and engage. For recognizing and wrestling with inequities and bias, see Safiya Umoja Noble, *Algorithms of Oppression: How Search Engines Reinforce Racism* (New York: New York University Press, 2018). See also Ruha Benjamin, *Race After Technology: Abolitionist Tools for the New Jim Code* (Cambridge: Polity, 2019).
9. For more on GenAI as a collaborative co-intelligence, see Ethan Mollick, *Co-Intelligence: Living and Working with AI* (New York: Portfolio/Penguin, 2024).
10. The scholars Trudi Jacobson and Thomas Mackey introduced the term "metaliteracy" in 2011 and further developed the concept in their published works. See especially Thomas P. Mackey and Trudi E. Jacobson, *Metaliteracy: Reinventing Information Literacy to Empower Learners* (Chicago: American Library Association, 2014); *Metaliteracy in Practice* (Chicago: American Library Association, 2016); *Metaliterate Learning for the Post-Truth World* (Chicago: American Library Association, 2019); and *Metaliteracy in a Connected World: Developing Learners as Producers* (Chicago: American Library Association, 2022).

PART II
Strategic Implementation of AI in Libraries

4

The AI Integration Process

USE, ADOPTION, IMPLEMENTATION, INTEGRATION: CLARIFYING OUR LANGUAGE

As you explore the ever-changing dialogue and research landscape related to generative AI, you will encounter a broad spectrum of language that appears particular but is often deployed interchangeably: use, adoption, implementation, and integration. We want to offer at the outset of this chapter a brief explanation of how we think about the nuances of each of these terms.

Use. This is the most straightforward of these terms. "Use" indicates whether or not we deploy or engage AI in our work. We either do or we don't use AI.

Adoption. This term suggests a conscious decision about current and future engagement with AI in our work. This is really about our relationship, and more specifically about our premeditated and proactive relationship, to artificial intelligence. While use might occur "just because," adoption is always an intentional choice. We will talk more about the importance of adoption in the next chapter.

Implementation. This is the how and why of our use after adoption. Implementation is the intentional and strategic application of the technology, tools, and practices that we adopted for use in our ongoing work.

Integration. This term describes the ways in which AI becomes an integral, and eventually inseparable, part of our work. After having implemented AI, we are able to experience its applications fully and completely.

We could argue, then, that our use informs our decision to move toward adoption, that adoption enables and empowers our implementation, and that implementation is the essential step that precedes the integration of artificial intelligence fully into our work as libraries and librarians.

WHY SHIFTING FROM ACCESS TO ADOPTION IS ESSENTIAL FOR LIBRARIES

Libraries, by their very nature, are some of the most carefully curated collections of information and learning in the world. With their meticulous organization, highly skilled professionals, and generous welcome of all people, libraries and librarians have understood and enabled *access* for generations. But we are also aware that access alone is insufficient for the kind of transformation and connection we are hoping for. It is not enough that the library exists; it must also be used to reach its full potential.

The challenges and opportunities we face in the coming years as AI becomes more deeply integrated into our world are similar. For the full benefit and potential of this technology to be realized in a way that serves all people in ways that bend toward justice, equity, and inclusion, we must understand that access alone is insufficient. Fortunately, libraries are better prepared for this moment than most other institutions, and certainly more than you might realize.

But what is more than access? We believe that this is adoption, the ability not only to access these technologies but also to understand and choose how they are integrated into our lives with enough skill and proficiency to benefit from them. This shift beyond access to adoption is crucial for three reasons.

If libraries only enable access, they will become redundant or obsolete. While it has been true in the past that access to information, technology, and the internet was far from equitable (and there is certainly much more work to be done here), most state-of-the-art AI tools are public, free, and available on mobile and desktop devices. For most people, access to them through the library will not be essential.

This is in perfect alignment with the values and work of libraries and librarians. Because we believe that literacy is a human right and that it serves the common good, because we believe that diversity, equity, and inclusion are not only matters of justice but of our collective human flourishing, and because we know that access to information is essential to economic and social welfare, we can see that this is our time to claim the center.

Those who are unable elsewhere to acquire the access and skills necessary for adoption will be left behind. It is important that we are honest and clear-eyed about the economic and employment implications of the rapid advance of artificial intelligence. We must recognize that many people whom the larger system does not sufficiently help to navigate this steep disruptive curve will need the kinds of support, training, and modeling that libraries and librarians are optimally positioned to provide.

A FOUR-FOLD FRAMEWORK FOR AI INTEGRATION

There are four essential concepts that we must consider and leverage as we think about the ongoing integration of AI into our work. These concepts serve as a kind of orientation, a grounding that helps us to navigate the rapidly growing impact of artificial intelligence on the work of libraries and librarians and the needs and concerns of those we serve. These are by no means the only things that we need to consider, but they can function both as a starting place and a litmus test for our choices as we continue to respond to the future that unfolds in front of us.

Human-Centered

As we have already made clear, being human-centered is not merely a crucial part of our approach to artificial intelligence; it should be the starting place and guardrail for any and all decisions that we make. Specifically, the commitment to being human-centered leads us to ask the question: *What does this do to and for human beings?*

We should pose this question not only about a technology or specific tool or use case itself but also about the decisions that we make as individuals, as institutions, and as a profession. It is important to note that within this question there are two distinct locations of inquiry, *to* and *for*. And while these are undoubtedly related, it is not uncommon that there is a kind of tension between the two.

It is clear from leading-edge work on generative AI that the ways in which we engage with information will change drastically in the near future. This is especially true as these generative tools become increasingly sophisticated, accurate, and publicly available. Here, we should specifically ask our two questions: What does this shift in capability and expectation do *to* human beings (e.g., will it require up-skilling or re-skilling, will it lead to job loss, etc.)? And what does this shift in capabilities do *for* human beings (e.g., will it unlock accelerated discovery and innovation, increase productivity, increase income, etc.)? It is important to recognize that we will not always receive a positive response to both of these questions, but we must be keenly aware of the answers to both of them, especially as we work to align those answers with our commitment to the nurture, care, and flourishing of human beings.

Metaliteracy

Metaliteracy is neither new nor controversial for libraries and librarians, but it is a crucial piece in helping endow people with the skills needed to navigate the future of our shared life as it is increasingly permeated by artificial intelligence. While we touched on this in chapter 3, and we will explore what it means specifically for navigating the future of AI and libraries in chapter 7, it is enough here to understand that metaliteracy as a part of this framework leads us to ask the question: *What and how do we need to learn in order to move into our desired future?*

This question, while it can feel abstract, is not bound to a distant time horizon. The desired future may be the solution to a current problem that needs to be resolved as quickly as possible. Or, the desired future may be part of a larger vision, mission, or goal of which this moment is an incremental yet important contribution.

The primary focus of this question, though, is not about time but about content and approach. The question is an invitation to ask about the raw materials, the wisdom, experience, and expertise that we need to access or acquire. Where can we find them? From whom can and should we learn? And once we have answered this initial question, then we begin to inquire about our approach to that information: At what level of complexity and concentration should we engage?

Right Tool, Right Job

One of the common challenges when people are attempting to solve problems or enhance their learning and work with artificial intelligence is when we choose the wrong tool or the wrong approach and then we extrapolate that "failure" to AI as a whole. This is the source of much of the perception that "AI can't do much," when in reality it is a mismatch of the tool(s) to the job.

"Right tool, right job" is really an invitation to consider the approach and the appropriateness of our work and how artificial intelligence might be a part of that work. It is essential that we understand that the utilization of AI tools only works if both of these components, right tool and right job, are in place. Doing the right job with the wrong tool leads to suboptimal or even damaging results. Using the right tool in the wrong way contributes to underperformance or even counterproductive results in our work.

The Jagged Frontier

The metaphor of the "jagged frontier" emerged from a research paper published by the Harvard Business School that explored two interconnected realities: First, the paper noted that the complexity of a task is not always an indication of whether or not it lies within the boundaries of the capabilities of available AI tools. Second, it noted that the frontier of what is possible moves unpredictably, unevenly, and frequently, thus producing a "jagged frontier."[1]

These twin insights demonstrate that we should take two things into account with our AI implementation going forward. What is possible *right now* is always a temporary reality. There is no indication that we are anywhere close to any kind of "wall" in gains in the capabilities of these tools. What you cannot currently do, you should be capturing and attempting again in the future. As these tools advance or as additional tools and use cases emerge, you should revisit your own personal "jagged frontier" and see if the boundaries of what is possible to you have moved. This is how it will be from now on.

NAVIGATING STAKEHOLDER ENGAGEMENT

Libraries and librarians operate at the center of many stakeholders, ones both internal and external to their organization. It is essential as we navigate the disruptions and possibilities that are emerging from generative AI that we intentionally and constructively engage with all stakeholders.

In these early days of navigating AI in and around library spaces (and these are the very earliest of days), it is helpful to think of stakeholders as both vertical, those within our organization, and horizontal, those connected to but external to our organization.

While there are lots of complicated dynamics here, it is important that we avoid three common approaches to stakeholder engagement that, while they may be effective with other issues, are counterproductive when it comes to integrating AI into the life and work of libraries and librarians. After exploring each of these briefly, we will introduce an alternative, which we call the "convening approach."

Top-Down Approach

The top-down approach often utilizes hierarchies that are already present in the organization to produce, release, and implement the integration of AI across the team. As it relates to integrating AI, there are three immediate weaknesses to this approach:

1. It results in a concentration of power, not necessarily a concentration of wisdom and expertise. Someone's current role or influence within your organization is no indicator of their capacity or contribution to navigating the emerging disruptions posed by AI.
2. This approach can push out other voices that can provide really important contributions from their wisdom, and it can increase suspicions of how AI will shape and reshape the work of libraries and librarians. A top-down approach almost never has room for any kind of perspectival diversity.
3. There is little or no room for horizontal, external stakeholders to engage. In this approach, they are most often simply presented with an invitation to get on board or move on.

Ultimately, this approach suffers from a lack of organizational agility, and an exclusion of additional perspectives that are not often or not yet involved. It basically operates as if the organization itself is the predominant or even the exclusive concern. These three vulnerabilities are likely to adversely impact how libraries and librarians navigate the generative AI frontier in their work.

Sequential Approach

This approach operates more like concentric circles or ripples in water, in which decisions flow from an initial ring of decision-makers outward to the rest of the organization. This is not to be confused with a gradual approach, but rather it is a posture that aims to tackle questions about AI integration sequentially, from the center to the periphery. This approach is susceptible to two serious flaws:

1. It increases the likelihood that counterproductive assumptions, understandings, and practices will be "baked in" to the approach before those with additional perspective, experience, and expertise can contribute. It is this preemptive limitation of input that can create headaches later.
2. This approach very quickly diminishes any capacity for ongoing learning and development by limiting the capacity for such work to the bandwidth, availability, and interest of your initial ring of participants. This means that as your implementation grows and spreads across your organization, the agility and responsiveness of your approach become more and more cemented and inflexible.

Ultimately, this approach often discovers too late that there are real changes that the initial participants could or should have made but which they will now have a disproportionately difficult time implementing.

Voluntary, Opt-In Approach

On the surface, this approach seems welcoming, open, and agile. Its appearance of welcome and flexibility is often misunderstood as a constructive approach, but in practice it suffers from two major problems:

1. By its very nature, this approach prioritizes the early adopters, the techno-optimists, and the tech-savvy members of the organization. This is not bad, but it tends to dis-incentivize those who are skeptical, not tech-savvy, or who are Luddite or "old school" in their approach. This lack of diversity in perspective, experience, and approach is counterproductive.
2. This approach ignores that generative AI is an *arrival technology*, meaning that it will impact our lives and work whether we opt in or not, in much the same way that electricity was integrated into our lives in the

early twentieth century. This kind of "if you want to join us" approach conveys a sense that generative AI's impact will not be as big or as fast as it most certainly will be (and already has been).

This kind of hands-off approach to engaging with generative AI ultimately leaves no one really in control of the work, thus diminishing its potential and its results.

THE CONVENING APPROACH

The approach that we believe is most effective is what we describe as a "convening approach." This approach leverages the ability of libraries and librarians to cultivate and sustain a multi-stakeholder process that facilitates real, lasting impact. This approach utilizes the participation of those in positions of power and influence (similar to the top-down approach). In this approach, people throughout the organization can determine their proximity to the work (like the sequential approach). Finally, it brings together a much more complex and diverse group of perspectives, experience, and expertise, hopefully all founded in a shared commitment to the future (like the voluntary, opt-in approach).

THE CONVENING APPROACH AS GRAVITATIONAL AGENCY IN ACTION

The convening approach represents a tangible manifestation of libraries' gravitational agency across all three spheres of influence. It transforms abstract principles of human-centered AI integration into concrete practices that shape institutional cultures and community engagement with these emerging technologies.

At the personal level, the convening approach empowers individual librarians to act as nodes of connection within their organizations. When a children's librarian invites teachers, parents, and educational technology experts to discuss AI literacy for young learners, or when a systems librarian brings IT staff and public service colleagues together to evaluate a new AI-powered discovery tool, they exercise personal agency beyond their formal role. This personal convening power enables librarians to amplify their gravitational influence, creating spaces where diverse perspectives can interact and inform better decisions.

At the institutional level, the convening approach enables libraries to exercise agency by establishing themselves as trusted mediators in complex technological conversations. Rather than passively implementing technologies developed elsewhere or reactively responding to changes, libraries become active orchestrators of thoughtful implementation. By convening cross-functional teams spanning hierarchical levels and departmental boundaries, libraries create gravitational fields where innovation, caution, enthusiasm, and critical thinking can productively coexist. This institutional convening power transforms libraries from service providers to strategic partners and guides in navigating technological change.

At the ecosystem level, the convening approach mobilizes libraries' collective gravitational influence to shape broader societal conversations about AI. When library associations convene multi-stakeholder dialogues involving technology developers, policy-makers, educators, and community representatives, they position the library ecosystem as a crucial nexus for ethical AI development and deployment. These convenings create generative spaces where technological possibilities are grounded in human needs and values, with libraries as the gravitational center that both holds these conversations together and moves them toward constructive outcomes.

The convening approach is effective precisely because it leverages libraries' unique position between and below—between diverse stakeholders and below the surface of technological change. It harnesses libraries' gravitational influence not through mandates or directives but through creating dynamic, human-centered spaces where meaningful dialogue, collaborative decision-making, and agency can emerge.

The convening approach consists of three essential elements:

1. *It is grounded in shared values aimed at human-centered objectives.* This approach is driven by its commitment to the *how* and the *why* of our work, especially whenever the *what* and *when* are difficult to ascertain with any certainty. Values (the how) and objectives (the why) must be understood as inseparable from each other. This is because values alone can turn us into idealists who are detached from and even disinterested in the real world; and objectives alone, even human-centered ones, can turn us into utilitarians who are focused on the ends of our work in malformative ways.

2. *It is built from a foundation of a commitment to universal basic literacy.* A convening approach not only allows but also actively cultivates a diversity of perspectives and reactions to generative AI in the work of libraries and librarians. In order for this to move beyond an unhelpful "us versus them" mentality, it must be grounded in a shared understanding, familiarity, and basic level of proficiency and literacy in generative AI. We have to be able to talk *to* each other or we will inevitably talk *past* one another.

3. *It is committed to the work over the long term and beyond the walls of our institution.* The convening approach values stakeholders, both vertical and horizontal, and even those from outside the library community who share our values and objectives in anticipating and building the future that we wish to inhabit. The work of AI integration cannot be a short-term project because we are not talking about incremental or incidental change here but a fundamental transformation of the ways in which human learning and work operate. This means that we must be invested in this work on an ongoing basis. Second, we must be willing to learn from those outside of our institution because the speed, scale, and scope of these shifts are far too broad and consequential for us to be "reinventing the wheel" in our libraries time and time again.

The convening approach embraces the library's role as a center of gravity. Serving as conveners enables libraries and librarians to be both the centripetal and centrifugal forces of gravity, preserving an ecosystem that is committed to human flourishing and learning, and propelling us forward in the construction of a more equitable, beautiful, and nurturing world for the entire human family. Exerting ourselves as the center of this shift through our explicit and unapologetic commitment to our human-centered work is an indispensable contribution to our shared life and future.

CREATING A ROAD MAP FOR AI INTEGRATION IN YOUR LIBRARY

To really get started on the work of AI integration in your library or library ecosystem, there are three essential *first* moves that you need to make. These should be done thoughtfully, carefully, and with a commitment to documenting your process in order to help you both remember and reflect going forward.

Identifying a Cross-Functional Team That Is Deep and Wide

When building out the initial participants in your convening approach to AI integration, it is essential that this team be *cross-functional*, *deep*, and *wide*. Each of these elements serves an important purpose that helps to cultivate a generative and sustainable group for this work.

Cross-functional. It is important that the group of individuals who help lead this effort in your library and beyond come from a variety of roles within your institution. This diversity of both experience and current work will better enable you to navigate the complexities and pervasiveness of AI integration. This is not just a public service issue, an administrative issue, a technical issue, or a human capital issue; it is all of these things and more. But this kind of role diversity is insufficient for the task at hand. We must also go wide and deep.

Wide. We have all witnessed or participated in projects, committees, and other forms of collaboration that have a span of roles and perspectives yet fail in any meaningful way to be actually representative. It is essential that you are mindful of those roles and voices in your institution that are typically excluded or minimized in important conversations and that you work to resolve this at the earliest stages of the work.

Deep. It is also important to recognize that often our selections even across a wide variety of roles and departments still regularly adhere to a kind of reinforcement of hierarchies of power and authority. This can be particularly disadvantageous in this work because it is not always the most experienced and authoritative voices that can most contribute to work at the cutting edge, where what is coming and what we will do in the present are largely yet to be determined. If we are not careful, constructing a cross-functional team that is wide but not deep will merely entrench and exacerbate some of the long-standing challenges and obstacles that we have encountered in previous major disruptions of our shared work.

Why the team must be cross-functional, wide, and deep. We must remember that generative AI presents the most disruptive and consequential shift in the practice and potential of human learning in all of history. We are talking about an acceleration of scale, scope, and systems of knowledge curation and production that has never been possible before. The teams that we assemble to begin navigating this work will have a disproportionate influence on the results of that work going forward. The truth is that we don't know all of the skills, experience, expertise, and intuition that will be necessary to build the future that we want and need with generative AI. This is why the development of this kind of team as the initial center of gravity is so crucial.

Identifying Core Values as Grounding, Not Guardrails

Throughout this book, you will find us talking about values as both a foundation and driving force in the work of AI integration for libraries and librarians. It is important here that we talk about *how* we use values. Oftentimes, without intentional efforts to prevent it, values can become a kind of "red line"—something we don't meaningfully consider until they have been violated. In this way, they ultimately function as a kind of passive guardrail. We don't really utilize them unless we are at risk of stepping outside of their boundaries. The inevitable result of such an orientation to values is that they become performative instead of generative.

Instead, we must think of those core values that should serve as the grounding of our work. These are an animating force, the center, the fuel of our shared labor to build a world for ourselves and for others. It is important that your team take time to identify and articulate your core values. This serves as both a form of reflection and accountability. It can serve to convene the kinds of stakeholders, both vertical and horizontal, who are needed to move into our yet-to-be-determined future. Make your values clear, make them explicit, and make them the core of your identity and work.

Identifying Goals Specific to Your Organization

Finally, it is important to understand that every library or library ecosystem is unique, with its own particular strengths, vulnerabilities, constraints, and opportunities. This means that any kind of one-size-fits-all approach is only assured of one thing: fitting no one.

To more clearly identify your organization's core services and goals, you might ask:

- What are the essential day-to-day things that we do in the library and for whom?

- Where do we find gaps between the needs we are aware of and the resources (physical, relational, economic, etc.) that are necessary to at least begin to address those needs?
- What are the services that are important to our work but are at risk or have already been reduced due to constraints or decisions that have impacted us?

By asking these and other questions, we will be able to think more clearly not only about the services that we currently offer but also the entire breadth of services that we would like to recover, cultivate, or expand in our specific context.

When thinking about core needs, we might ask questions like:

- What are the limitations of budget, infrastructure, or personnel that have most directly impacted our work as librarians and a library?
- What other kinds of resources might better enhance our opportunity to pursue the work we wish to do for those we serve?
- What do we as librarians need to be better prepared for the important but undoubtedly taxing work that we do every day?

When we have a better understanding of our core services, our core needs, where we are currently, and where we would like to be going forward, we are positioned to do one of the most important things that generative AI has made possible for us: to *imagine* and *work* toward a new future.

JUST THE NEXT STEP

In this new era for libraries, and for all of us, it is important that we not get too hung up on detailed, long-term plans and road maps. This is why we believe it's so important to get really clear on the values that drive our work. The timelines for the full impact of generative AI are hard to predict, but they will almost certainly be faster and more pervasive than many of us imagine. So please do not take all this as an invitation to craft a comprehensive five-year strategic plan. Quite the opposite. The best plan for today, and going forward, is to put in place a durable infrastructure that encourages us to collaboratively work toward a human-centered future even as we find out, in real time, what that actually looks like. Don't get caught up in trying to plan all of your next steps. Instead, get serious about the kinds of people who you will work with as you take the next step, and the next step, and the step after that. Moving in this way, librarians are positioned to enhance not only their own work but also the world and life that we all share.

NOTE

1. Fabrizio Dell'Acqua et al., "Navigating the Jagged Technological Frontier: Field Experimental Evidence of the Effects of AI on Knowledge Worker Productivity and Quality," Working Paper 24-013, Harvard Business School, 2023, www.hbs.edu/ris/Publication%20Files/24-013_d9b45b68-9e74-42d6-a1c6-c72fb70c7282.pdf.

5

A Framework for AI Adoption

We have talked about how AI integration should be human-centered, and in the previous chapter, we explored why we have to move in this direction. Now we want to offer some ways to think about *how* exactly we might do this. We also hope to explain why too many times, especially as it relates to the integration of technology to advance our work, libraries have experienced less than ideal results.

In the previous chapter, we talked about AI *integration*, but here we want to take a step back and talk about what must happen before meaningful and sustainable integration can occur: that is, AI *adoption*.

IMPLEMENTATION IS NOT ADOPTION

One of the most common mistakes when it comes to integrating new technology into our work is to conflate implementation with adoption. Oftentimes, the implementation of technology works something like this: First, the new technology (software, hardware, or use case) is made available and is turned on. Second, the users, whether they are interested in it or not, are given some basic form of instruction or information, and that's it! We have successfully arrived at "implementation."

This has been true of our experience with technology in many parts of our lives, like the introduction of self-checkout at the grocery store, the electronic banking that saves us a trip to a branch location, and the use of automated customer service systems when we really just need to chat with someone for a few brief moments. We essentially act as if Access + Information = Implementation is the whole process.

But as we navigate the integration of generative AI in our libraries and our work, we must not make this same mistake. It is one thing to introduce or implement a new technology into a library, but it is quite another thing for people to *actually start using that technology and accept it*. This is what we mean by "adoption." What we are aiming for is more than a change in what is available for those we serve; we are aiming for a change in behavior and intention, both in ourselves and in our users so the new technology we implement is used and accepted to the fullest extent that is beneficial.

This kind of change often encounters real resistance, sometimes grounded in our preference for the things we are the most comfortable with. This is our nostalgia for a time in which we no longer live—the "good ole days"—or even from some of our deeply held values. It is important to remember that we have already navigated many significant technological shifts in our lifetime, and though they felt jarring in the moment, we now take them for granted. We anticipate that in some ways we will experience this AI technological change in the same manner; that is, intense responses in the earliest days and increasing levels of use, adaptation, and acceptance as time goes by.

We might look back and remember the life of libraries when not only the card catalog was analog but the entire collection was as well. We might think back to what librarianship was like before the internet, or what helping people to develop information literacy was like before social media appeared. Whatever we do in integrating AI's disruptive technology in our learning and work, it is clear that mere implementation is not enough. It must be accompanied by adoption: that is, widespread and everyday use and acceptance.

A TECHNOLOGY ADOPTION MODEL: UTAUT2

Because we are talking about adoption, which is more substantive and sustainable than mere implementation, it is important to explore briefly what we believe to be the most helpful technology adoption model as it relates to generative AI and libraries. There are many, many technology adoption models out there, but in our work we utilize the "*unified theory of acceptance and use of technology 2*" (UTAUT2)[1] model for a number of important reasons:

- The UTAUT2 model takes seriously both the external factors that motivate technology adoption (e.g., its social value, its economic advantages, and the ways in which it may positively affect our performance) and the internal factors that are unique to each individual (e.g., how we personally feel about technology use in general, questions of trust, our internal motivation, and our cultivation of habits).
- The model helps make clear that knowing *how* to use a technology is insufficient to ensure that it is used effectively.
- The model understands that the adoption of technology is ultimately about changing behavior, and that the process by which this happens and is sustained requires thoughtful and intentional learning and work.

We won't go into all the details about the particularities of the UTAUT2 model for a couple of reasons. First, when you examine the literature on this model, particularly as it relates to AI, you will find that the model is utilized in numerous ways, with fine-tuned approaches in nearly every case. Thus, presenting a one-size-fits-all approach to this model is counterproductive. Second, the insights that we draw from this model (which inform the remainder of this chapter) do not come from any rigid adherence to its design, but from meaningfully engaging with its insights into habit formation and behavioral change and its implications for sustained and sustainable adoption.

THREE FAILED APPROACHES TO LEARNING AND DEVELOPMENT

Before we can get to the work of adoption itself, we have to name three ways that institutions have approached the learning, professional, and personal development needs of those who lead and those we serve. These help us to better understand how we have an opportunity to do something different, and ultimately better, going forward.

No one left behind. This approach is focused on those who are lowest or last in a learning community. The entire learning community is focused on the desire to be approachable, helpful, and concerned about those for whom learning is difficult or problematic. This approach, well-meaning though it may be, undermines the ability of somewhat more advanced learners to progress and leaves them unequipped to move forward. It also ignores advanced learners altogether.

Aim for the middle. This approach tries to orient itself to the "average" learner, the center of the bell curve. The hope is that the presentation is within the "stretch" capabilities of the least advanced learners, while advanced learners will just go with the flow, knowing that they can't be the real focus of that learning opportunity. In this approach, the appeal to the average gives you just that, more of the average.

The frontier is everything. This approach takes the entirely opposite position with its "catch up or die trying" posture. Here, the instruction is aimed explicitly and often exclusively at the most advanced students. Perhaps it is within the "stretch" capabilities of slightly less advanced learners, but that would be merely an added benefit, not an intended outcome. Learners who are the lowest and last are excluded intentionally. In this approach, we have a conflation of complexity with quality and rigor.

The kind of learning users are entitled to should not be determined by the information they have or how deeply they understand it. These three approaches overlook this point, especially if the goal is to bring all learners to a shared level of basic understanding.

AN APPROACH TO LEARNING BY INTEREST AND READINESS

An approach to building and delivering our instruction is to measure learners' interest and readiness, and together these two indicators can help us create instruction that is approachable, meaningful, and effective. Let's consider interest and readiness separately, and then look at what happens when we consider them in combination as we prepare our instruction for those we lead and those we serve.

Interest. This is an indicator of curiosity and a desire to learn and engage. It is a measure of openness to what one has not yet mastered and a commitment to the acquisition of experience and skill. This attitude toward the new and unknown exists on a spectrum; it can change, sometimes very quickly, with experience, and it can be unpredictable.

Readiness. This is an indicator of skill, capacity, and capability. It is more objective and stable than interest. It is a measure of familiarity, proficiency, and competency. This attitude toward something new and unknown also exists on a spectrum, but it is less subject to emotions, and the learners' ability to improve their readiness is largely incremental and predictable.

Why We Must Consider Both Together

If we asked you to recall a time when you were very capable of doing something but had *zero* interest in actually doing it, we imagine that you could remember one relatively quickly. Perhaps it was a project at work where they were looking for volunteers, or it was your least favorite task around the house, or some other moment when you were capable but had to be almost forced to get it done.

In the same way, we imagine that it would be just as easy to recall a time when there was something that you most certainly wanted to do, but your interest far outstripped your ability to actually accomplish it. For example, I may love to watch a great baking or cooking competition, but my skill set wouldn't get me very far in such a competition.

Taken alone, neither interest nor readiness are capable of telling us how ready we are for the kinds of learning and adaptation that generative AI, or any kind of new and substantive learning, will require of us. It is only when they are in combination that we are able to effectively appreciate our *starting point* toward our objective.

The Interest and Readiness Matrix

An "Interest and Readiness Matrix" might look something like the one shown in figure 5.1.

INTEREST

CURIOUS NOVICE high interest + low readiness	**ACTIVE EXPLORER** high interest + high readiness
CHOSEN HOLDOUT low interest + low readiness	**DETACHED PARTICIPANT** low interest + high readiness

READINESS

FIGURE 5.1
The Interest and Readiness Matrix

In figure 5.1, the Active Explorer is the person who is both motivated and capable. Because they possess both interest and readiness, they are uniquely positioned to rapidly enhance their skills and capabilities. The Curious Novice is the kind of person who is able and willing to put in the work but doesn't yet have the skill needed to really advance their own learning and is thus dependent on others to get them where they need to be, at least initially. The Chosen Holdout is uninterested or perhaps even antagonistic and has no skill or capability to move forward. You will find a lot of anti-advancement sentiment in this quadrant, even though the details of those roots of suspicion can be complex and multifaceted. Finally, the Detached Participant is someone who has the skill and capability to advance their own learning, and may in fact already be advanced, but for whatever reason is not interested in capitalizing on their abilities in this regard. This can be the case for any number of reasons, but it is not uncommon for these people to be the most resistant of all stakeholders.

Locating Yourself in the Interest and Readiness Matrix

It is important to properly locate someone in this matrix because this will shape that person's particular journey toward the kind of basic literacy and proficiency that is needed to adopt AI integration in their personal work, in the library, and in the larger ecosystem. This can be done in a kind of self-study or in a very basic instrument to measure interest and readiness can be utilized.

The important thing to remember here is that wherever a person locates their type in the matrix, this is not a classification, a scarlet letter, or a badge of honor but merely a *starting place* to help them most effectively learn and engage in the work of AI adoption.

Why the Matrix Is Important

There are four major reasons why the Interest and Readiness Matrix is helpful in preparing individuals and institutions for AI integration in a conscious learning process aimed at AI adoption.

A commitment to an equity of outcome. The entire design of the matrix is grounded in the commitment to bring everyone to a shared level of literacy and proficiency. The destination is the same, but this system operates with the understanding that each person's route to this shared conclusion is unique and requires a kind of pedagogy and design that is tailored to their particular needs and strengths.

Targeted content progression. Understanding where someone fits on the matrix enables us to design and deploy learning experiences that give everyone what they need *in the order they need it.* This level of specificity and customization can help us achieve better and more equitable learning outcomes.

Honoring of individual particularity. It is not necessarily a liability when someone lacks readiness or even interest, just as it is not necessarily an asset when someone already possesses those qualities. Instead, our attention is not on who is more or less prepared or positioned for this learning but on the work we do toward our shared destination, which is literacy and proficiency for the entire team.

More effectively scalable. This approach enables us to avoid the three failed approaches to learning that we discussed earlier, where we overly focus on the least prepared, the average, or the most advanced learners to the detriment of others. Our approach is also more scalable because it enables a more rapid and intentional pace of learning in which each group is differentiated so different learners receive precisely what they need.

FOUR ELEMENTS OF AI ADOPTION

When we think about the learning that is necessary for basic literacy and proficiency in generative AI, there are four essential elements that must be part of the work: grammar, habit, skill, and motivation. As we will see shortly, the ways in which these are delivered and enacted are dependent on where one is located in the Interest and Readiness Matrix, but all four elements are universal. These four categories are the what, when, why, and how of learning that leads to AI adoption and ultimately to integration.

Grammar

Grammar is the shared language, the foundational understanding of the terms, ideas, processes, and concepts that are essential to AI integration for librarians and libraries. This is what we need first and foremost to be able to more effectively build our skills, communicate with others, and engage both vertical and horizontal stakeholders. A shared grammar is one of the primary ways that we learn to work together, to navigate this work as prophets, priests, and curators, and to do so in ways that don't talk past one another, but with one another as colleagues and collaborators grounded in common values that lead to human flourishing.

Habit

Habit is about both our choice and ability to integrate skills and abilities into our routine activities. Habit is an indication that someone has acquired some level of proficiency in such a way that it becomes part of their behavior. Habits are not always constructive, however, and so we're not just interested in habit formation but in the formation of good and generative habits. Helping people to realize how certain grammar, skills, and motivation work together to enhance what is possible is essential for the kind of habit formation that is beneficial to both the individual and the collective.

Skill

Skill is the ability and capacity to accomplish a desired outcome. This is the part of our learning that becomes more complex and more sophisticated over time, though the difficulty of that learning curve is unique for each person and level. Skill is the most objective of the four categories, with its demonstration being the primary form of assessing one's own learning.

Motivation

This is perhaps the most intangible of the four elements, but it is also the key to sustainable adoption. We have all experienced the erosion of our habits and skills when motivation is lost, and we have often seen how a lack of motivation can adversely affect the learning process. In this way, we understand that motivation, some of which is internal to the person and some of which is external in nature, is essential to the long-term outcomes and viability of our learning and work.

A LEARNING DESIGN FOR THIS FRAMEWORK

We recognize that everyone begins at their own position as it relates to interest and readiness, and we understand that when it comes to AI adoption, we must cultivate grammar, habit, skill, and motivation. But what is the underlying design by which we create and deliver this kind of differentiated learning that brings us to a shared destination? Here, we introduce the Learning Design Framework (figure 5.2).

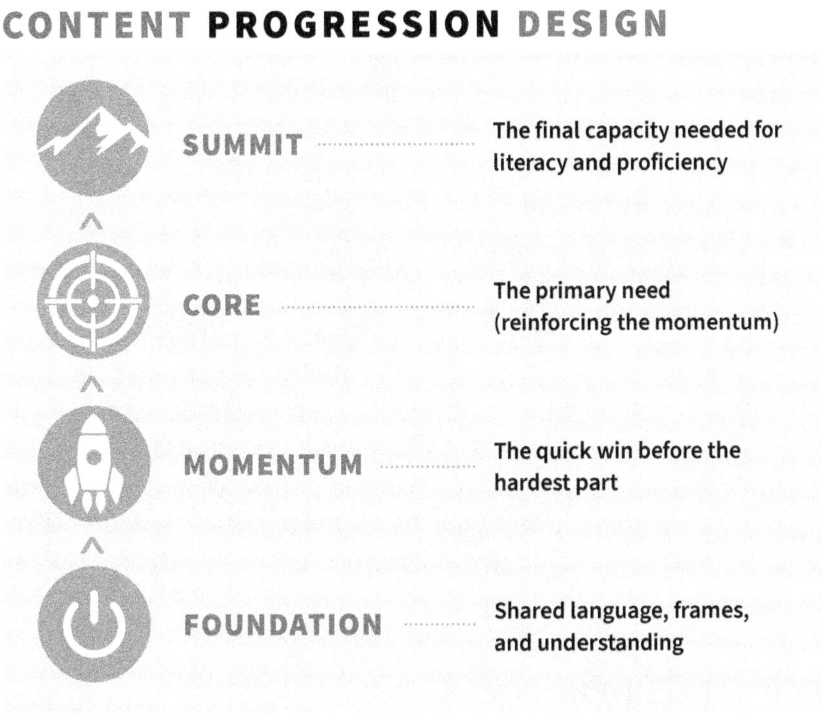

CONTENT PROGRESSION DESIGN

SUMMIT — The final capacity needed for literacy and proficiency

CORE — The primary need (reinforcing the momentum)

MOMENTUM — The quick win before the hardest part

FOUNDATION — Shared language, frames, and understanding

FIGURE 5.2
Learning Design Framework

Foundation: Shared Language, Frames, and Understanding

Here, everyone begins with grammar. A shared language, framing, and understanding are essential to all future learning. Without this common understanding, this stable floor from which to build, it is likely that the entire structure will collapse. And while some people need more foundational support than others, we must raise all participants to a level of excellence in this area before proceeding further with any learning toward adoption.

Momentum: The Quick Win Before the Hardest Part

This is where the differentiation really begins. Here, we begin by playing to our learners' strengths, by enabling and celebrating some early wins, and by providing the affective, social, and internal environment to ensure that they are capable and prepared to continue their learning. As we will see, what part of the framework fits in this position is unique, but its role is the same: to provide energy and momentum for what comes next.

Core: Reinforcing the Momentum
This is the hardest part of the work. Here, we test our endurance, our commitment, and the strength of our learning community to enable us to continue. In this phase, we tackle the largest or most complex gaps in the individual's learning. This is why the foundation and momentum are so important; they are the essential fuel for this difficult work of facing our greatest vulnerabilities and challenges as they relate to our learning.

Summit: The Final Capacity Needed for Literacy and Proficiency
This is not the most difficult work, but without it the launch into doing the work will be premature and will suffer from unnecessary friction, breakdown, and a failure to meet our hopes and expectations. The summit is the last piece of the puzzle, the key that unlocks the door, and the switch that turns on the light. This is not the time to ease up but the time to blast off and propel the learner to the next level of their newly developed and earned competency and proficiency.

BRINGING IT ALL TOGETHER

So what does it look like to bring together the Interest and Readiness Matrix, the four elements of AI adoption, and the Learning Design Framework? It looks something like figure 5.3.

Everyone starts with grammar. This is essential to provide a robust and shared foundation, one that enables us to build well going forward and enables people across the institution to collaborate even when they navigate different learning paths to a common destination. After this shared foundation, each group and individual begin their own, differentiated path.

Active Explorer. The quick and early win for the individual who is both interested and capable involves the acquisition of additional levels of skill. Capitalizing on what we already bring to the table helps provide energy and momentum for the difficult work ahead. Habit is the core need for the Active Explorer and can be difficult work, as people who are both engaged and competent often rely on their skill and skip habit formation altogether. This makes for less sustainable adoption and leads to a loss of potential benefits down the road. Finally, the Active Explorer completes their initial learning with additional work in motivation, which facilitates the ongoing development of skill and habit going forward.

Chapter 5: A Framework for AI Adoption | 75

	FOUNDATION	MOMENTUM	CORE	SUMMIT
ACTIVE EXPLORER	Grammar	Skill	Habit	Motivation
CURIOUS NOVICE	Grammar	Motivation	Skill	Habit
DETACHED PARTICIPANT	Grammar	Habit	Skill	Motivation
CHOSEN HOLDOUT	Grammar	Motivation	Habit	Skill

FIGURE 5.3
In combination: Interest and Readiness Matrix, the four elements of AI adoption, and the Learning Design Framework

Curious Novice. The quick and early win for those who are interested but lack skill and experience is to concentrate on *why* they are engaging in this form of learning and up-skilling. Here we leverage their interest and curiosity to build momentum for the difficult work of building out their skills. The core need of skill comes through intentional, focused effort to understand this new technology. With their newly acquired skill, the Curious Novice is able to cultivate the final piece of their formation, the development of habit.

Chosen Holdout. The quick and early win for those who lack interest and readiness is to build some motivation, to help them understand how the adoption of generative AI can enable them to do more of the work that is meaningful to them. From here, it is important to begin to build habit, as skill development will be a more extensive process. The Chosen Holdout should recognize that habit formation is the essential tool for long-term and sustainable skill-building. Once they are grounded in the work on grammar, motivation, and habit formation they have already done, they will find themselves better positioned to hone and acquire additional skills going forward.

Detached Participant. The quick and early win for what is often the most resistant participant is to accelerate and enhance their current skill set.

Leveraging that high level of readiness is an important source of energy for the hard work the Detached Participant must do in building motivation. In their core work, these learners must cultivate some form of motivation to continue moving forward. The Detached Participant may require a number of different approaches to motivation, whether an internal one (it benefits one's own work) or an external one (it helps the people one serves). Finally, the combination of enhanced skill and motivation is the groundwork for robustly cultivating and sustaining our habits.

WHY THIS WORK MATTERS

There are three reasons why it is important to be intentional in the way we shape our colleagues and our institutions to navigate the coming world made possible by generative AI. First, we will only get one opportunity to navigate this work at the cutting edge. Any work after this, say in a couple of years, will be either an attempt to "catch up" or a repetition of the work that we've already done for people who are new to our teams or institutions. In other words, how we navigate this frontier is a unique opportunity and will have real consequences for our work in the near and not-so-near future.

Second, as libraries have known for a long time, the way that we educate people matters, especially as we seek to cultivate and sustain a world that is good for the whole human family. This commitment to navigating the work in a way that is explicitly and unapologetically human-centered is not only a defining feature of librarians and libraries but also an asset to the larger work of traversing the disruption and opportunities posed by generative AI.

Finally, this kind of framework provides us with a reproducible process for engaging in all kinds of formation and information. Thinking meaningfully about the affective, social, and skills-based starting points of those we engage is a useful perspective for maximizing the impact of all of the education, advocacy, and support that librarians and libraries offer day after day.

CONCLUSION

When it comes to generative AI, we are looking for more than simply providing access and a little support; we are looking at how to navigate the work toward adoption and ultimately toward integration. The gap between implementation and adoption is significant, and the consequences of which of these we prioritize can be substantial. If we are committed to enabling the greatest number of people possible to take maximum advantage of this technology for their informational, vocational, and economic flourishing, then it will have to be a carefully designed and enacted process that moves us toward adoption.

This is important for librarians and libraries in particular because historically we have been marginalized when it comes to adopting these kinds of technological innovations. This often stems from one of two factors: either because of cost-cutting measures applied to libraries that already occupy a marginal place in their institution or community (at least in the minds of those who hold the money); or because those people fundamentally misunderstand the value, impact, and results of the work that librarians and libraries do each and every day. No matter which of these attitudes has led to the shrinking footprint, budget, and staffing in our libraries, they are both misinformed ones, and if allowed to continue, they will almost certainly hasten the kinds of budgetary and personnel cuts that have been the trend for some time now. The rise of artificial intelligence is, literally, a once-in-a-lifetime opportunity for libraries to assert themselves at the center of the most profound technological shift in human history. If history is any indication, we will most certainly not be invited to the table, at least not as the leaders, conveners, and experts that we are. It is up to us in this moment to claim the center.

NOTE

1. There is an extensive body of literature about the UTAUT2 model in relationship to both higher education and applications of artificial intelligence (though not always explicitly about generative AI). While this literature does not specifically mention libraries, one can easily extrapolate the impact and insights of this technology adoption model to those contexts. See, for example, the following materials: Mohammed Alhwaiti, "Acceptance of Artificial Intelligence Application in the Post-Covid Era and Its Impact on Faculty Members' Occupational Well-Being and Teaching Self Efficacy: A Path Analysis Using the UTAUT 2 Model," *Applied Artificial Intelligence* 37, no. 1 (December 31, 2023): 2175110, https://doi.org/10.1080/08839514.2023.2175110; Irfan Ali and Nosheen Fatima Warraich, "Use and Acceptance of Technology with Academic and Digital Libraries Context: A Meta-Analysis of the UTAUT Model and Future Direction," *Journal of Librarianship and Information Science* (June 8, 2023), 096100062311797,

https://doi.org/10.1177/09610006231179716; María García de Blanes Sebastián, José Ramón Sarmiento Guede, and Arta Antonovica, "Application and Extension of the UTAUT2 Model for Determining Behavioral Intention Factors in Use of the Artificial Intelligence Virtual Assistants," *Frontiers in Psychology* 13 (October 18, 2022): 993935, https://doi.org/10.3389/fpsyg.2022.993935; Jashwini Narayan and Samantha Naidu, "A New Contextual and Comprehensive Application of the UTAUT2 Model Post-COVID-19 Pandemic in Higher Education," *Higher Education Quarterly* 78, no. 1 (2024): 47–77, https://doi.org/10.1111/hequ.12441; Viswanath Venkatesh, James Y. L. Thong, and Xin Xu, "Consumer Acceptance and Use of Information Technology: Extending the Unified Theory of Acceptance and Use of Technology," *MIS Quarterly* 36, no. 1 (2012): 157–78, https://doi.org/10.2307/41410412; and Liangyong Xue, Abdullah Mat Rashid, and Sha Ouyang, "The Unified Theory of Acceptance and Use of Technology (UTAUT) in Higher Education: A Systematic Review," *SAGE Open* 14, no. 1 (January 2024): 21582440241229570, https://doi.org/10.1177/21582440241229570.

6

The Unseen Cost and Possibilities of AI Integration

As we wrap up this part of the book on the practical steps involved in AI integration, we want to briefly explore five elements that librarians and libraries should consider as they engage within their institutions and with stakeholders around generative AI—(1) the "work behind the work," (2) the robust infrastructure and process, (3) the human side of technological change, (4) a culture of continuous learning and adaptation, and (5) budget and resource allocation. The way that each of these elements operates will be unique to your particular context, so we hope these initial recommendations can serve as a starting point that will guide your work going forward.

UNDERSTANDING THE "WORK BEHIND THE WORK"

One of the things that gets left out of too many conversations about engaging and integrating generative AI is that there is an entire set of skills and competencies necessary for success in this work that has nothing to do with the technology itself. We call these the "work behind the work."

We came to this understanding upon observing that the skills we needed to acquire our professional expertise (and thus become librarians) were often different than the skills we needed to leverage that expertise once we had acquired it. We see this all the time in other areas of life as well. We have probably all had teachers who knew their subject matter very well but were not very good at teaching it. Or we saw people who were very good in one particular application of their skills, but when they tried to apply those same skills in a different way, they met with less impressive results. Think about a sports coach who used to be only a mediocre player, or a practitioner who did their job really well until they were promoted into management. These are all well-documented phenomena, but we don't often stop to ask ourselves what causes this to happen.

For librarians and libraries, the "work behind the work" is intimately bound up with skills that are so essential to the work of librarianship that they have become nearly automatic. What is important for us to recognize is that these skill sets, while "normal" and common to librarians, are not nearly as common elsewhere. For example, public librarians have incredible abilities when it comes to knowledge management. Organizing, arranging, and efficiently locating information are some of the core skills of anyone in our field, but you don't have to look hard anywhere else to find out that such skills are rare indeed. Librarians know that information literacy is important, but its value is matched only by how rare it is to find it "in the wild."

For librarians, there are many elements of the "work behind the work" that we make explicit for the stakeholders that we engage and serve. These skills position libraries to serve as centers of gravity for very large and complex ecosystems within their institutions and beyond.

Here are some of the skills and abilities that typify the "work behind the work" we do as librarians:

- *Information architecture.* Librarians have an incredible capacity to classify, organize, and manage information across the full spectrum of human learning. As generative AI enables increasingly complex and interdisciplinary forms of inquiry, this skill will become even more valuable.
- *The question(s) behind the question.* How often has someone asked your assistance in finding something when you knew that the thing they needed was not what they were asking for? The ability of librarians to see "behind" and "through" an inquiry to better understand its deeper, more foundational, or more generative nature can be crucial when it comes to leveraging generative AI to enhance human learning.
- *Knowledge translation.* The ability of librarians to translate complex and sophisticated information into accessible formats has been central to our work, whether we are talking about LibGuides, reference guides, or curated collections of texts and information. In the world of human learning using generative AI, this power, which is usually new to everyone else, will be dramatically enhanced and accelerated for librarians and libraries.

- *Process management.* Librarians and libraries have a long history of providing organized yet flexible and responsive systems and approaches that serve people with consistency and quality. As the rest of the world begins to realize that understanding an underlying process is crucial for leveraging generative AI, librarians and libraries are already prepared to capitalize on this capacity.
- *Community engagement.* Who has a deeper tradition of building spaces of welcome, inclusion, and support for all people than librarians? The fundamentally human-centered approach of our work gives us immense skill to embody and model community engagement for others as we navigate the frontier of learning and work.
- *Continuous adaptation.* We don't do librarianship like we used to, and that's okay. What we have shown in the course of every technological change is that librarians and libraries are resilient, adaptable, and able to navigate rapid and substantive change while staying true to our values and commitments. Others will need to learn this same kind of grounded flexibility going forward.
- *Knowledge preservation and management.* We are about to embark on an explosion in human learning where the scope, scale, and speed of that learning will increase exponentially. How will we be able to capture, structure, and leverage all of this new learning, and who can help us imagine how we will do that? Librarians and libraries are poised to lead here in ways for which others have absolutely no capacity.

These are just some of the ways that the "work behind the work," those invisible skills that are essential to our success, must come to the forefront and be made visible. And it must be made clear that the best place for everyone to acquire these skills in a world shaped by generative AI is the library—from those who have always possessed these same information and knowledge skills.

DEVELOPING A ROBUST INFRASTRUCTURE AND PROCESS

One of the ways that librarians can make themselves indispensable to their institutions and beyond is to develop, document, and deploy a robust infrastructure and process for these "hidden" skills and their work on the integration of generative AI.

Libraries, by their very nature, have several important pieces of infrastructure that provide great value going forward:

- *Physical infrastructure.* This includes spaces for learning and gathering, access to technology and the internet, and access to physical collections and other sources of information.
- *Human infrastructure.* This is the wisdom, experience, and expertise of your team both individually and as a collective, which provides power and possibility for human-centered work.
- *Geographic location.* Libraries are often located at strategic sites in a community (for public libraries), an institution (for academic libraries), or some other type of entity (for special libraries).

In addition to these kinds of infrastructure, librarians and libraries stand to benefit from the work of consciously and explicitly documenting the work they do in integrating generative AI. We often focus on doing the work to pursue our goals without documenting the processes that are involved. This lack of documentation makes librarians appear to accomplish their work through "magic" or some kind of inherent competency. This inability to tangibly demonstrate *how* they get the work done makes it harder for libraries to do two interconnected things:

1. *To advocate for themselves.* A focus on outcomes without the documentation of how we arrived at those results makes our requests and demands for additional funding and support look abstract and aspirational, when they are actually a reflection of the quality and quantity of our contributions to the work.
2. *To enact this wisdom, experience, and expertise elsewhere.* As good as librarians and libraries are at the things we mentioned in the previous section, it can be profoundly disheartening and frustrating to watch others in our institutions struggle or fail because of decisions, or the failure to make decisions, that librarians and libraries would have been easily able to anticipate or navigate. This means that the work of translating our tacit knowledge into something concrete and tangible can unfold in spaces that lack the background, training, and skills that are so natural to libraries.

FOSTERING A CULTURE OF CONTINUOUS LEARNING AND ADAPTATION

Like all other institutions, librarians and libraries exist on a spectrum when it comes to ongoing learning and development. There are those of us who long for and try to protect the way we've always done things in the past, while others among us try not only to keep up with change but also to participate in the leading edge themselves. And all the while, many librarians find themselves somewhere in the middle between these two poles.

Librarians and libraries have a long history of learning and adaptation, and this has served us well as we navigated changes in our own work throughout our lifetime. It is now important for us not only to enhance and sustain this orientation in our institutions but also to work toward its expansion into all areas of the world where we live, work, and exert influence. Librarians and libraries have not only a great contribution to make here but also a profound obligation to lead in building space for the ongoing learning, re-skilling, and up-skilling that will be necessary in the near future for many of us.

MANAGING THE HUMAN SIDE OF TECHNOLOGICAL CHANGE

In our commitment to human-centered engagement with generative AI, it is important to recognize that we are not only responsible for what is merely a technical process of adoption and integration; our work is fundamentally and inseparably connected to the real lives, real identities, and real complexities of human beings. This means that there are some things that we need to get clear about as we navigate this frontier in an unapologetically human-centered way.

Efficiency and productivity should not be our primary concern. The work of a librarian is deeply tied to a sense of vocation and identity. As we figure out how generative AI will fundamentally change our work, we must be conscious of how people's sense of vocation and identity are impacted. While it might be tempting to look first at the places where efficiency and productivity can be achieved most rapidly and extensively, this alone is not a sufficient reason to make these changes. We must also ask, often explicitly to the affected individuals, how such shifts would impact them.

There is undoubtedly work that is tedious and time-consuming that inevitably pulls us away from work that is more engaging, more interesting, and more connected to others. But we should ensure that in our rush to accelerate or even automate the former that we don't unintentionally or unconsciously harm someone's sense of vocation or identity as a librarian. If we find that there is tension or the potential for harm in the way that someone relates to their work, then we must carefully and thoughtfully try to determine how much of this is preference, personality, and mere discomfort with change, and how much of it would strip away some of the connective work that is so important to us and our colleagues.

We must look for ways to reallocate our time and bandwidth. Automation will be a real and profound consequence of the advance of generative AI in libraries. This will significantly change the way and the speed with which we accomplish our work. AI is already doing so, and there is no reason to assume that this will do anything other than accelerate and expand going forward. But this does not mean that we can do *less*. It's not as if we will be able to reduce our hours or diminish our resources for the people we serve simply because we can do the same amount of work, or more, in a way that is better and faster than before. Instead, we must think about the impact of automation as an invitation to reallocate our time, energy, expertise, and emotional labor into other work. This is not to suggest that we should try to squeeze more out of every workday, and merely expand the demands of our already overly full to-do lists. Instead we should think more fundamentally about what can be possible with these changes in our work. What are the areas in which we wish we were able to invest more time, energy, and attention? What kind of connective, relational work do we wish was more feasible under our current conditions, and how could we leverage the changes to move in that direction going forward?

We must consciously and explicitly refuse to use the changes and advances in our work as mere tools for additional extraction; we must instead work to explore opportunities for us to more meaningfully center human beings—both those of us who work in libraries and those who benefit from our services.

BUDGET AND RESOURCE ALLOCATION FOR AI INITIATIVES

Budgeting and allocation is a particularly complex and dynamic area, especially when we consider the diversity of libraries and the institutions and communities they serve. What we want to offer here is not a line-item proposal for what the coming fiscal years should look like but the kinds of underlying questions and inquiries that can help you discern what your budgeting and allocation can and should look like in your specific context.

Budgetary Allocation

There are a couple of unique dynamics that relate to our historical experience of technology and library spaces and what we are confronted with in generative AI.

Quality does not always come at a premium. Historically, the best models, features, and capabilities, particularly as this relates to digital technology, have been restricted to those with the requisite capital to purchase and maintain access to that technology. The cutting edge was available, but it was unevenly distributed among those who could or could not afford access. What we are seeing with generative AI is that very capable, very high-quality tools offer at least some meaningful and useful access at low or no cost, making equity of access increasingly possible. There are also real opportunities for libraries to acquire leverage with some of these companies so as to create spaces for partnership and collaboration that will level the playing field even further.

Experimentation does not have to be at the enterprise level. Undoubtedly the companies making the kinds of tools that leverage generative AI are more than happy to sign deals that come with multi-year, institution-wide access. But we are still in the experimental stage for determining whether or not a particular tool meets the specific needs and expectations of libraries, so there is rarely a need for anything that is either long-term or expensive. Many of the leading tools that could and will be leveraged in libraries can be engaged experimentally with individual licenses that are inexpensive and do not require any kind of long-term commitment.

Efficiencies and savings should be reinvested in engaging generative AI. Generative AI offers great potential for changes and developments in the work of librarians and libraries that can free up capital which has previously been allocated to other tasks. This is not to suggest that we should reduce our human capital in libraries, but to recognize that the time and cost of some of the work will be changed by these tools and technology.

Libraries should be willing and committed to the acquisition of additional capital. We know that librarians are often averse to extending services that cost money as part of their commitment to equity of access, and this is an important motivation. But as we move forward, we should also recognize an opportunity that is presented here: Those organizations with capital (e.g., foundations, institutions, industry, etc.) that need to learn from the wisdom, experience, and expertise of librarians and libraries are able to contribute capital, which can in turn serve to expand library services to those for whom cost would be a barrier. The acquisition of financial resources for libraries does not run counter to our deep and important commitment to equity of access and service but can in fact enhance it.

Resource Allocation

Here, we are talking about the non-budgetary resources of librarians and libraries. This is primarily about the time, energy, and attention we devote to our work. We understand that libraries do not have an excess of these precious commodities. Between essential services, special projects, and any added responsibilities, it is much easier to *imagine* how we might spend our time otherwise than what is actually feasible. What you will find in the following section are some strategies and approaches to incrementally lean in to this work of resource allocation that can be empowered by generative AI.

Identifying Opportunities for Impact and Connection

One way to identify new opportunities is to get really clear about those areas where generative AI may have the most dramatic initial impact or might make room for deeper, wider, or more meaningful connections with others. This could include areas where you wish there was a greater investment of time, energy, and attention, or ones where there is a lack of those resources that demand our attention and remediation. Here are some concrete examples of the potential impact and connections arising from our engagement with generative AI:

- *Working with members of the public looking for employment.* This is undoubtedly an important and potentially time-consuming service that is important for the well-being of those seeking support from the library. Here, we might ask how generative AI might help these individuals more effectively navigate the process of looking for work, whether that is more compelling cover letters, richer explanations of previous experience and present skills, or up-skilling and re-skilling that enable them to apply for additional job opportunities.
- *Assisting students with research.* In academic and public libraries, this is a vital contribution to students and learners of all kinds. Librarians

and libraries' engagement with generative AI could enhance their ability not only to serve more individuals in this way, but also to pass along more advanced and effective research skills that could help them beyond their encounters in the library.

- *Tackling mundane and repetitive tasks.* There are certainly parts of our work that are huge consumers of our time, attention, and energy and are either mundane or repetitive. And they can be a major drain on other more important, more interesting, and more connective work as well. Generative AI could help us spend less time on work in areas like inventory management, data entry and organization, and reporting, and thus make a real contribution to our being able to pursue more vital elements and areas of our work.

So if our colleagues or our library are already stretched to the limit in their duties, conducting a thought exercise might help us imagine ways in which AI tools and technology could enable us to make positive changes in the workplace. While there may not yet be a capacity to *act*, at least initially, there should be sufficient space to *inquire*, to try and learn from others both within and beyond librarianship whether such developments are feasible and, if so, how they might be implemented.

If you find that there is some space to do more than simply inquire, we encourage you to ask three questions here:

1. What changes would bring the most relief if we were able to implement them?
2. What changes would have the most impact on our ability to more fully use our values, skills, and expertise for the benefit of our colleagues and those we serve?
3. Where can we learn from people who are already doing this work? We should recognize that reinventing the wheel is not only counterproductive but perhaps even harmful to the work that we hope to accomplish.

LIBRARIES AS HUBS FOR AI INNOVATION

What might a kind of convening approach look like? One way we might think about this is to create what we call an "innovation hub." Innovation hubs are centers where stakeholders and different communities can gather to imagine, develop, and shape the future. As AI innovation hubs, libraries could serve as active participants in determining how AI will be integrated into society, creating environments where ethical considerations, community needs, and technological capabilities converge to inform policy and practice. Through frameworks like STACKS and transparent approaches to AI implementation, libraries could demonstrate how institutions can balance innovation with responsibility, setting standards that influence policy development at all levels.

INNOVATION HUBS: GRAVITATIONAL AGENCY MADE VISIBLE

Innovation hubs represent the physical and programmatic embodiment of libraries' gravitational agency. They transform our metaphorical role as centers of gravity into tangible spaces and initiatives where our stabilizing, connecting, and energizing forces become visible and accessible to our communities. Through these hubs, libraries exercise agency across all three spheres—personal, institutional, and ecosystem—in ways that make abstract principles concrete.

At the personal level, innovation hubs empower librarians to become agents of technological change rather than merely responding to it. Within these spaces, librarians develop their own emerging AI expertise and cultivate their capacity to guide others, expressing personal agency through demonstration, instruction, and consultative services. A librarian who helps a small business owner understand how AI might transform their customer service or assists a student in critically evaluating AI-generated research is exercising personal gravitational agency—drawing others into ethical and effective engagement with these technologies.

At the institutional level, innovation hubs enable libraries to shape organizational and community approaches to AI integration. By creating dedicated spaces for experimentation, learning, and critical dialogue, libraries exercise institutional agency that influences how their broader communities understand and adopt AI technologies. These hubs become institutional manifestations of the library's gravitational pull—physical centers where diverse stakeholders are drawn together to explore, question, and collaborate around emerging technologies. Through them, libraries move from reactive service providers to proactive shapers of technological culture.

At the ecosystem level, networks of innovation hubs across different libraries amplify collective gravitational agency. When public, academic, school, and special libraries create complementary innovation initiatives tailored to their specific communities but connected through shared values and approaches, they establish a distributed yet unified field of influence. These networked hubs enable the library ecosystem to exert gravitational force at scale, creating consistent yet contextually appropriate guidance for AI adoption across society. Through professional associations and collaborative networks, libraries can share resources, strategies, and outcomes from their innovation hubs, strengthening their collective impact.

What makes these innovation hubs distinctly library-centered is their grounding in our core values and positional authority. Unlike corporate innovation labs focused primarily on product development or academic research centers concerned mainly with theoretical advances, library innovation hubs operate from our unique position between diverse stakeholders and below the surface of technological implementation. These hubs harness our tradition of user-centered service, our commitment to equity and accessibility, and our expertise in information organization and literacy to create innovation spaces that are inherently human-centered and ethically grounded.

This positioning enables library innovation hubs to serve three essential functions that express our gravitational agency:

- *Convene*: Bring together diverse stakeholders to:
    » Share knowledge and perspectives about AI
    » Develop ethical frameworks for AI implementation
    » Address community needs and concerns

- *Connect*: Foster relationships that:
    » Bridge technological capabilities with human needs
    » Link individual learning with community benefits
    » Connect local initiatives with broader movements

- *Catalyze*: Spark transformative change by:
    » Promoting AI literacy across communities
    » Supporting ethical AI innovation
    » Building toward a positive future

These roles represent an evolution of libraries' traditional functions, not a departure from them. The values that have always guided libraries—access, privacy, intellectual freedom, and service to the community—now inform our approach to AI integration.

UNLEASHING THE IMAGINATION OF LIBRARIANS AND LIBRARIES

Ultimately, we hope that this approach will enable librarians and libraries to unleash their imagination—and to envision a future in which their work is not devalued or underappreciated but is held up as a valuable contribution to the future of learning and work for the human family. There are undoubtedly real constraints on our time and resources, but we must be bold and assertive with the future that we envision and the contributions that we can make to our shared life.

We want to invite you to think strategically and seriously but to also understand that the horizon of what is possible in the near future is much wider, bolder, and more exciting than we previously imagined. Few if any of us could have anticipated even five years ago what would be possible now, much less what is going to be within reach for us very, very soon.

We want you to imagine and begin building a future for libraries where the following are true:

- Libraries and librarians are better understood and appreciated as "the strong one under the floor" that they have always been.
- Libraries and librarians are given access to more financial and institutional resources as stakeholders recognize the full breadth of the human-centered and information skills that are native to librarianship.
- Libraries and librarians are increasingly consulted for wisdom and guidance in the larger ecosystems in which they participate and are finally given their rightful seat of influence at the table where decisions are made.
- Libraries and librarians are enabled to better care for one another and the people they serve in ways that were previously limited or unavailable to them.

All of these things can be true, but they all require libraries to *claim their place*. It will require an assertiveness, a boldness, and a willingness to claim a role that has not always been easy or automatic for us. But this pivot, the willingness to claim the center, is essential not only for the future of libraries but also for the well-being of the human family as we navigate all of the changes, opportunities, risks, possibilities, hopes, and anxieties that come along with generative AI technology.

This is our moment, a moment like we have never seen before—and may never see again—in which to claim a central role in the Age of Intelligence.

PART III

The Future of Libraries in the Age of Intelligence

… 7

Metaliteracy

Exploring the Intersections of AI and the ACRL Framework

In an era of artificial intelligence, literacy must evolve beyond traditional skills-based frameworks to encompass a more dynamic, integrated approach to learning and understanding. As described in chapter 3, metaliteracy provides this broader framework, offering a comprehensive model that unites cognitive, metacognitive, behavioral, and affective domains in the service of deeper learning and engagement. By emphasizing reflective thinking and adaptive learning across multiple literacy types, metaliteracy enables learners to move beyond skill acquisition to develop the self-aware, critical consciousness that is essential for navigating the information ecosystem in the Age of Intelligence.

This metaliteracy framework proves particularly valuable as we consider the integration of AI literacy with existing information literacy concepts. The ACRL Framework for Information Literacy for Higher Education (or ACRL Framework), with its emphasis on threshold concepts and broader understanding, already embodies many metaliteracy principles.[1] It acknowledges that true literacy involves knowing how to find and evaluate information, and understanding the larger contexts and implications of information creation, dissemination, and use. As we extend this framework to encompass artificial intelligence, metaliteracy offers crucial insights into how learners can develop the multiple competencies needed to thrive in an AI-enhanced world.

The four domains of metaliteracy—cognitive, metacognitive, behavioral, and affective—map naturally onto the challenges and opportunities presented by AI integration in libraries. The cognitive domain supports an understanding of AI systems and their implications; the metacognitive domain enables critical reflection on AI interactions; the behavioral domain guides practical skill development; and the affective domain helps learners navigate the emotional and social dimensions of technological change. Together, these domains provide a foundation for the seven frames of AI literacy we propose in this chapter, while informing our understanding of how libraries can best support AI literacy development.

> In the past decade, no catalyst has emerged with greater potential to unite libraries across ecosystems than AI literacy.

This chapter examines how metaliteracy enriches our approach to AI literacy instruction and integration. We explore the gravitational relationship between durable skills, established literacies, and emerging AI competencies and consider how metaliteracy enables movement and interaction between these elements. Throughout, we position libraries as observatories and outposts on the jagged frontier of AI development, empowered by metaliteracy principles to guide their communities toward a thoughtful, ethical, and effective engagement with AI.

AI literacy is the seedbed from which a new era of library services can flourish, nurturing a profound integration and synergy across our field. We can position ourselves at the center of an evolving information landscape by recognizing AI literacy as a natural extension of the durable skills and multi-literacies that have long been at the heart of library instruction. We can claim a central role in an AI-literate society by cultivating AI literacy as a core competency that we develop and deepen for those we serve.

AI LITERACY AS AN ORIENTING, ETHICAL PRACTICE

An ethical engagement with AI exemplifies metaliteracy in action. It requires not just a cognitive understanding of ethical principles but metacognitive reflection on our choices, a behavioral implementation of ethical practices, and an affective awareness of how AI impacts individuals and communities. This multi-domain approach enables deeper ethical reasoning and more thoughtful AI integration.

Developing a comprehensive framework for AI literacy is, at its core, a human-centered activity that reflects our values and commitment to serving our communities. While it has ethical dimensions, it primarily represents our professional responsibility to equip people with the tools they need to navigate an AI-enhanced world thoughtfully and effectively. It represents our stance on how AI should be understood, evaluated, and utilized in our communities and offers a practical manifestation of our ethical commitments. This framework aligns with our human-centered paradigm and builds upon the foundational literacies that libraries have championed for decades. In this way, it bridges present understandings of librarianship with the AI-enhanced future we aspire to create, where libraries across the ecosystem are crucial centers of gravity in an AI-literate world.

THE FOUNDATION: MULTILITERACIES AND DURABLE SKILLS

AI literacy doesn't emerge in isolation; it exists within a complex system of multiple literacies that librarians have been mapping and exploring for decades. Across the library universe, professionals chart diverse constellations of literacies—information, digital, media, visual, and more. At the core of this system are durable skills like critical thinking, information discovery, and ethical reasoning. These skills form the gravitational center around which AI literacy revolves.

AI literacy intersects with existing literacies in a complex, interconnected system:

- *Information literacy*: This is the cornerstone of AI literacy. It equips users to evaluate AI-generated content critically and to understand AI training processes, much like they do when assessing traditional information sources.
- *Digital literacy*: This is the gateway to AI interaction. Proficiency in digital environments is crucial for effectively engaging with AI tools, including understanding data privacy and security implications.
- *Media literacy*: This evolves to encompass AI's role in content creation and distribution. It is vital for recognizing AI-generated or manipulated media in an era of sophisticated misinformation.
- *Data literacy*: This is the language of AI. Understanding data collection, analysis, and interpretation is essential for grasping AI processes and outputs.

- *Computational thinking*: This is the logic behind AI. While not universally taught in libraries, it helps in understanding AI algorithms and problem-solving approaches.
- *Visual literacy*: This expands to interpret AI-generated visuals. It's crucial for both understanding and creating content in an AI-enhanced visual landscape.
- *Maker literacy*: This shifts the role of learners from consumers to creators. AI empowers learners to create and innovate with various technologies.
- *Ethical literacy*: This is the moral compass of AI use. It guides humans-as-agents in navigating the ethical implications of AI, from bias to privacy concerns.

These intersecting literacies demonstrate how AI literacy does not exist in isolation but emerges from and contributes to a broader ecosystem of competencies. The metaliteracy framework helps us understand these relationships by providing an integrative approach that spans all four metaliteracy learning domains—cognitive, metacognitive, behavioral, and affective.

Metaliteracy's emphasis on the learner as both consumer and creator of information is particularly relevant to AI literacy, where users actively collaborate with AI systems to produce new content and insights. The 2025 Metaliteracy Goals and Learning Objectives explicitly acknowledge this relationship with objectives like "Evaluate the role of AI in shaping content while contemplating personal responsibility in ensuring ethical, accurate, and transparent engagement with its generation and impact" and "Develop ethical and creative approaches, both individually and collaboratively, to engage with AI to produce responsible content."[2]

By recognizing the foundational relationship between metaliteracy and AI literacy, libraries can leverage established instructional approaches and learning objectives while adapting them to address the unique characteristics of AI engagement. This continuity bridges libraries' traditional literacy instruction and emerging AI literacy needs, allowing for evolution rather than revolution in our approaches.

Librarians are uniquely positioned to guide AI literacy instruction by leveraging their expertise in these interconnected literacies. We must present AI literacy not as an isolated proficiency, but as an integral part of a broader ecosystem of durable skills and multiliteracies. This holistic approach will ensure that learners develop adaptable skills for use in our rapidly evolving technological universe. It frames AI literacy not as a revolution, but as a natural evolution of the critical thinking and information skills that have always been at the heart of librarianship.

The durable skills fostered by existing literacies form the gravitational core that keeps AI literacy in a stable orbit. They provide the fundamental forces of critical thinking, evaluation, and ethical consideration that are necessary for our communities to thrive in an AI-enhanced world. Aligning AI literacy with the ACRL Framework can provide a human-centered approach that energizes integration and instruction across library ecosystems, orienting our essential work for today and tomorrow.

SEVEN FRAMES OF AI LITERACY: A NEW PARADIGM

Building on the foundation of multiliteracies, we propose a framework for AI literacy comprising seven interconnected frames. These frames offer an orientation to AI for discerning its implications and potential in library contexts.

Overview of the Seven Frames

1. *AI development and use are ethical acts*: This frame emphasizes the moral implications of AI, prompting critical reflection on fairness, accountability, and AI's impact on human dignity and autonomy. The frame engages all four metaliteracy domains, requiring learners to understand ethical principles (cognitive), reflect on their choices (metacognitive), implement ethical practices (behavioral), and develop sensitivity to AI's human impact (affective).
2. *AI systems are constructed and contextual*: This frame highlights AI systems as human-made constructs, encouraging a critical examination of embedded assumptions and biases.
3. *AI operates within socio-technical systems*: This situates AI within broader societal contexts, exploring how it shapes and is shaped by social, cultural, and institutional factors.
4. *AI literacy is an evolving practice*: This acknowledges AI's rapid evolution, emphasizing continuous learning and adaptation. Metaliteracy's em-

phasis on adaptive learning and continuous reflection makes it particularly relevant to this frame, supporting learners as they navigate rapid technological change.
5. *AI is a collaborative co-intelligence*: This positions AI as a partner in problem-solving and creativity, thereby exploring human–AI synergy.
6. *AI literacy is empowering*: This connects AI literacy to digital citizenship and technological empowerment, enabling informed decision-making and public discourse participation.
7. *AI literacy deepens through reflective practice*: This frame stresses ongoing reflection on AI interactions, fostering metacognition and critical self-examination. It directly embodies metaliteracy's metacognitive domain while demonstrating how reflection enhances learning across cognitive, behavioral, and affective dimensions.

> When libraries position themselves at the core of AI literacy education, we become the gravitational center, providing the foundational support for our communities to navigate the Age of Intelligence's information landscape with confidence and critical acumen.

Relevance Across the Library Ecosystem

The framework that we propose applies to all library types—academic, public, school, government, and special—and can provide a conceptual model for instruction design, service development, and AI engagement across settings.

ALIGNMENT WITH THE ACRL FRAMEWORK FOR INFORMATION LITERACY

Our AI Literacy Framework intentionally echoes the ACRL Framework for Information Literacy, emphasizing transferable concepts rather than prescriptive skills. This approach ensures flexibility and adaptability, allowing librarians to tailor AI literacy instruction to their specific contexts and communities.

The alignment between our seven frames and the ACRL Framework reinforces the interconnected nature of AI literacy and information literacy:

1. *AI development and use are ethical acts*
   - » ACRL alignment: "Information Has Value"
   - » Emphasizes the ethical weight and societal impact of AI

2. *AI systems are constructed and contextual*
   - » ACRL alignment: "Authority Is Constructed and Contextual"
   - » Encourages the critical evaluation of AI systems and their outputs

3. *AI operates within socio-technical systems*
   - » ACRL alignment: "Information Creation as a Process"
   - » Extends this concept to AI development and deployment

4. *AI literacy is an evolving practice*
   - » ACRL alignment: "Searching as Strategic Exploration"
   - » Highlights the need for adaptability and ongoing learning in AI

5. *AI is a collaborative co-intelligence*
   - » ACRL alignment: "Scholarship as Conversation"
   - » Positions AI as a participant in knowledge creation and problem-solving

6. *AI literacy is empowering*
   - » ACRL alignment: "Research as Inquiry"
   - » Encourages an inquiring mindset toward AI and its societal implications

7. *AI literacy deepens through reflective practice*
   - » ACRL alignment: "Metacognition"
   - » Emphasizes critical self-reflection in AI interactions

This alignment underscores several key points:

- *Metacognition*: The ACRL Framework's focus on metaliteracy and metacognition is particularly relevant to AI literacy, emphasizing critical self-reflection in a rapidly evolving information ecosystem.
- *Interconnected concepts*: Both frameworks emphasize interconnected core concepts rather than prescriptive skills, recognizing the complex, contextual nature of understanding AI and information.

- *Adaptability*: The flexible nature of both frameworks allows for adaptation to various library contexts and evolving technological landscapes.
- *Holistic approach*: We promote a holistic understanding of the information ecosystem by integrating AI literacy with existing information literacy frameworks.

Our AI Literacy Framework, with its strong connections to the ACRL Framework, offers a timely and valuable resource for librarians across all library types. It provides a structured yet flexible approach to integrating AI literacy into existing information literacy programs, positioning libraries at the forefront of preparing communities for an AI-driven world.

THE EVOLVING NATURE OF THE AI LITERACY FRAMEWORK

Like the ACRL Framework, our AI Literacy Framework is designed to be dynamic and adaptive, mirroring the rapidly evolving landscape of artificial intelligence itself. This framework is not a static set of guidelines, but a living document that will grow and transform alongside technological and societal changes.[3]

Key aspects of the framework's evolving nature include:

- *Reflective adaptation*: The seventh frame, "AI literacy deepens through reflective practice," is a built-in mechanism for evolution. As librarians and learners reflect on their interactions with AI, new insights and needs will naturally emerge, informing updates to the framework.
- *Technological responsiveness*: As AI technologies advance, new ethical considerations, literacy needs, and societal implications will arise. The framework is designed to accommodate these changes, with each frame flexible enough to incorporate new developments.
- *Synergy with the ACRL Framework*: Our AI Literacy Framework is intended to evolve with the ACRL Framework for Information Literacy. As information literacy concepts adapt to new realities, so will our understanding of AI literacy.
- *Community input*: The framework will benefit from the collective wisdom of the library community. As librarians apply these concepts in various settings, their experiences and insights will contribute to the framework's refinement.

- *Interdisciplinary influence*: Advances in ethics, cognitive science, and human-computer interaction will inform the framework's ongoing development, ensuring that it remains at the cutting edge of AI literacy education.
- *Contextual adaptability*: The framework's flexibility allows for contextual adaptations across different library types and communities, with these adaptations potentially informing broader updates to the framework.

While our approach centers on the North American context, global perspectives will reveal that AI literacy is not a monolithic concept and requires a nuanced framework that is deeply influenced by regional technological ecosystems, cultural values, and educational infrastructures. Our framework provides a foundational model, but its implementation must be adaptable to diverse global contexts—recognizing that technological access, ethical considerations, and learning approaches vary significantly across different regions and educational systems.

By embracing this evolving nature, we ensure that the AI Literacy Framework can remain a relevant and powerful tool for librarians, adapting to meet the changing needs of our communities in an AI-enhanced world. The framework thus becomes a collaborative project that grows with the collective understanding of the library profession.

A GRAVITATIONAL MODEL FOR AI LITERACY INSTRUCTION

While the ACRL Framework provides a solid foundation, the rapidly evolving AI landscape demands a more dynamic and integrative model. Here, we introduce the "gravitational model of AI literacy," a three-dimensional representation of the interplay between foundational skills, diverse literacies, and emerging AI competencies.

The Structure of the Gravitational Model

1. *Core: Durable skills, ethics, and values*

    » This is the dense center of fundamental competencies (e.g., critical thinking, information discovery, ethical reasoning).
    » It acts as a gravitational center, stabilizing the entire system.

104 | Part III: The Future of Libraries in the Age of Intelligence

2. *Ground: Multiliteracies*

   » This is the rich layer surrounding the core (e.g., information literacy, media literacy, digital literacy).
   » It forms the context for more specific competencies.

3. *Atmosphere: Dynamic AI competencies*

   » This is the outermost layer of constantly evolving AI-specific skills.
   » It is represented as orbiting bodies, which reconfigure based on technological advances and use cases.

The gravitational model of AI literacy operates across three distinct but interrelated layers (figure 7.1). At its center, durable skills, ethics, and values act as fundamental forces—unchanging, ever-present capabilities like critical thinking and inquiry that influence everything in the system. These forces express themselves in the grounding layer as established literacy patterns—stable, recognizable frameworks like information literacy and media literacy that represent tested approaches to understanding and working with information. In the outermost layer, atmospheric elements represent dynamic

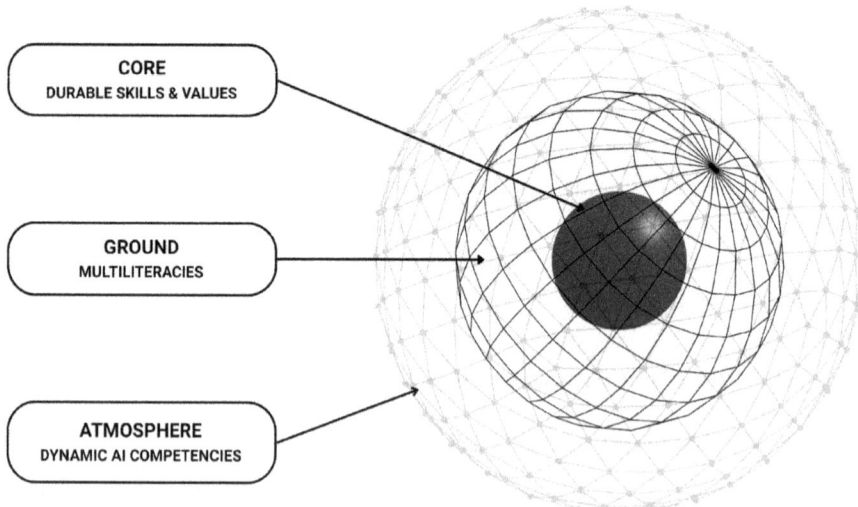

FIGURE 7.1
The gravitational model of AI literacy

competencies that emerge, evolve, and sometimes disappear in response to technological change. These elements are held in place by core skills but may shift position, reconfigure, disappear, or eventually become stable, grounded, and enduring.

Metaliteracy is the gravitational force that enables movement between layers and integration across domains. Its four domains—cognitive, metacognitive, behavioral, and affective—create the conditions for meaningful interaction between durable skills, established literacies, and emerging AI competencies.[4]

This gravitational model allows us to visualize several key aspects of AI literacy:

- The foundational nature of durable skills
- The contextual importance of established literacies
- The dynamic, evolving nature of AI-specific competencies
- The continuous interaction between all elements

This model empowers librarians to:

- Reinforce the pull of durable skills
- Cultivate a rich atmosphere of multiliteracies
- Guide the orbits of emerging AI competencies
- Orient learners for ethical AI use and integration

By conceptualizing AI literacy in this way, we can develop comprehensive, adaptable approaches to AI education and integration in libraries. The model emphasizes strong foundational skills while acknowledging the need for flexibility and continuous learning in the face of rapidly changing AI technologies. The gravitational model provides a frame for libraries to maintain their central role in information ecosystems while adapting to and shaping an AI-literate society. After all, the model reflects the core, durable skills librarians help develop, the multiple literacies that are the ground of our instruction, and the emerging AI-related competencies we aim to develop.

DURABLE SKILLS: THE GRAVITATIONAL CORE OF AI LITERACY

Durable skills comprise the gravitational core at the heart of our gravitational model. These fundamental, transferable competencies form the stable center around which multiliteracies and dynamic AI competencies orbit, providing a constant, unifying force in the rapidly evolving information landscape.

Key Durable Skills

- Critical thinking and analysis
- Information discovery and inquiry
- Synthesis and integration of complex ideas
- Communication (written, oral, visual)
- Collaboration and teamwork
- Adaptability and flexibility
- Creativity and innovation
- Ethical reasoning and decision-making
- Metacognition and self-reflection

Gravitational Properties of Durable Skills

- *Stability:* This provides a constant, reliable foundation for other competencies.
- *Transferability:* This enables navigation across various information contexts and technologies.
- *Attraction:* This connects and holds together different literacies and competencies.
- *Shaping force:* This influences approaches to information and technology interaction
- *Universal applicability:* This is fundamental to learning across all domains.

Durable skills reflect metaliteracy's integrated approach to learning. Critical thinking engages cognitive and metacognitive domains; collaboration involves behavioral and affective dimensions; and ethical reasoning requires all four domains to work in concert. This multi-domain engagement explains why these skills remain durable even as specific technologies change.

Librarians as Cultivators of Durable Skills

Librarians have long championed these fundamental competencies, fostering them through various instructional methods. In the context of AI literacy, this expertise translates directly into:

- *Information discovery*: The strategies for effective information-seeking remain crucial with AI tools.
- *Critical evaluation*: This is vital for assessing AI-generated content.
- *Ethical use of information*: This is directly applicable to responsible AI use.
- *Adaptability*: This is essential for engaging with evolving AI technologies.
- *Synthesis and integration*: This is key when combining AI-generated insights with traditional research.

By recognizing durable skills as the gravitational core of AI literacy, librarians can leverage their expertise to guide learners through AI's complex landscape. This approach ensures that AI literacy instruction builds upon a solid foundation of enduring, transferable skills.

In this model, librarians reinforce the pull of these durable skills, ensuring that as new AI competencies emerge and evolve, they remain grounded in fundamental information literacy principles. Durable skills thus form the substratum from which various literacies emerge and interconnect, reflecting capacities for accomplishing the "work behind the work" in academic, professional, and personal contexts.

MULTILITERACIES AS THE CONTEXTUAL GROUND

In our gravitational model of AI literacy, multiliteracies form the contextual ground or environment surrounding the core of durable skills. This ground provides the context in which specific AI competencies develop and operate.

Key Multiliteracies

- Information literacy
- Digital literacy
- Media literacy
- Data literacy
- Visual literacy
- Maker literacy
- Computational thinking
- Ethical literacy

Metaliteracy provides the integrative framework that enables these different literacies to work together cohesively, supporting learning across the cognitive, metacognitive, behavioral, and affective domains.

Characteristics of the Contextual Ground

- *Interconnected and overlapping*: In the contextual ground, these literacies blend and interact, creating a complex, multifaceted environment for learning and skill application.
- *Mediating role*: The ground translates fundamental skills into specific AI applications.
- *Evolving nature*: It adapts to emerging technologies and changing societal needs.
- *Foundational to AI literacy*: AI literacy builds upon and integrates with these existing multiliteracies.
- *Contextual lens*: The ground provides the framework through which AI tools and competencies are understood and applied.
- *Skill transfer facilitator*: It enables the application of skills across different literacy domains.
- *Grounded in core skills*: It remains anchored to fundamental competencies despite evolution.

By conceptualizing multiliteracies as our contextual ground, librarians can position themselves as key facilitators in developing the comprehensive literacy ecosystem that is necessary for effective AI engagement and integration. This approach recognizes the interconnected nature of various literacies and their collective contribution to AI literacy, enabling librarians to prepare their communities for the complexities of an AI-enhanced information landscape.

Implications for Librarians

- *Holistic instruction*: The contextual ground emphasizes the connections between AI literacy and other literacy domains.
- *Continuous learning*: It updates knowledge across multiple literacy areas to guide patrons effectively.
- *Service design*: It helps develop resources that support a comprehensive literacy ecosystem.

- *Advocacy*: It promotes a multifaceted approach to literacy education for AI readiness.
- *Community preparation*: It fosters multiliteracies to facilitate effective AI integration.

DYNAMIC AI COMPETENCIES AS AN ORBITAL ATMOSPHERE

In our gravitational model for AI literacy, dynamic AI competencies form the outermost layer, represented as constellations in an orbital atmosphere. This conceptualization captures the fluid, evolving nature of AI-specific skills and knowledge in a rapidly changing technological landscape.

Characteristics of Dynamic AI Competencies

1. *Nature*
   - Dynamic competencies are the skills and knowledge specific to AI technologies and applications.
   - They are rapidly evolving, mirroring the fast-paced development of AI.
   - Examples: Proficiency with specific AI tools, understanding of current AI algorithms, familiarity with emerging AI applications.

2. *Orbital representation*
   - The dynamic competencies symbolize constant motion and change.
   - Their varying "orbits" represent proximity to core skills or specificity to certain AI applications.
   - Constellations form as related competencies cluster around particular AI uses.

3. *Interaction with core and ground*
   - The interaction is influenced by the gravitational pull of durable skills at the core.
   - Core and ground interact with multiliteracies, gaining context and meaning.

4. *Configurable nature*
   » Constellations reconfigure based on specific needs, tasks, or emerging technologies.
   » This represents the adaptability required in AI literacy.
5. *Emergence and obsolescence*
   » New competencies emerge as new AI technologies develop.
   » Outdated competencies may "fall" back to the core or fade from relevance.

This conceptual model allows librarians to balance adaptability to rapid technological change with the cultivation of enduring foundational skills. Metaliteracy's emphasis on self-directed and reflective learning enables individuals to acquire and integrate new AI competencies as they emerge. This model positions libraries as dynamic institutions capable of guiding their communities in complex and evolving constellations of AI-related dynamic competencies.

Implications for Librarians

- *Strategic skill development* balances the cultivation of enduring skills with agility in dynamic competencies.
- *Resource allocation* invests in durable skills while flexibly acquiring dynamic competencies.
- *Adaptable instruction* creates frameworks that evolve with the AI landscape.
- *Long-term planning* informs libraries' services and professional development strategies.
- *Patron empowerment* guides the development of balanced skill sets.
- *Ethical grounding* navigates AI's ethical implications using enduring principles.
- *Continuous learning* emphasizes ongoing education, especially for dynamic competencies.
- *Interdisciplinary connections* foster cross-disciplinary approaches to AI literacy.

Distinguishing Durable Skills from Dynamic Competencies

The gravitational model emphasizes a critical distinction between durable skills at the core and dynamic AI competencies in orbit. Understanding this difference is crucial for effective AI literacy instruction:

1. *Permanence vs. Fluidity*

   » *Durable skills*: Long-lasting, foundational abilities that remain relevant across technological changes
   » *Dynamic competencies*: Fluid, evolving skills that are specific to current AI technologies and applications

2. *Breadth vs. Specificity*

   » *Durable skills*: Broad, transferable abilities that are applicable across various contexts
   » *Dynamic competencies*: Specific knowledge and skills that are tied to particular AI tools or applications

3. *Stability vs. Adaptability*

   » *Durable skills*: Provide a stable foundation for learning and application
   » *Dynamic competencies*: Require constant updating to keep pace with AI advances

4. *Investment Strategy*

   » *Durable skills*: Warrant long-term, in-depth development
   » *Dynamic competencies*: Require flexible, just-in-time learning approaches

5. *Instructional Focus*

   » *Durable skills*: Emphasize deep understanding and application across contexts
   » *Dynamic competencies*: Focus on practical application and rapid skill acquisition

By recognizing this distinction, librarians can:

- Design balanced AI literacy programs that develop both types of skills
- Help patrons understand which skills to focus on for long-term growth vs. immediate application
- Adapt instructional methods to suit the nature of each skill type
- Prepare patrons for continuous learning in AI while ensuring they have a solid foundation of enduring skills

ACTUALIZING AI LITERACY THROUGH THE GRAVITATIONAL MODEL

As we navigate the rapidly evolving landscape of artificial intelligence, the seven frames of AI literacy provide a crucial foundation for understanding and engaging with these technologies. These frames—emphasizing ethical considerations, contextual awareness, socio-technical systems, evolving practices, collaborative intelligence, empowerment, and reflective practice—offer a comprehensive lens through which librarians and patrons alike can approach AI literacy.

The seven frames of AI literacy don't exist separately from the gravitational model, but rather act as organizing principles that guide and shape how the entire system operates. While the gravitational model provides the structure—with durable skills, ethics, and values as core forces, multiliteracies as the contextual ground, and AI competencies as orbital, atmospheric elements—the frames provide the principles by which this structure functions. They explain how and why elements move between layers, how forces manifest in different contexts, and how the system evolves while maintaining stability. Together, they form a unified system where the frames provide purpose and direction while the model offers a concrete structure for understanding and implementing AI literacy. This integration enables libraries to approach AI literacy development systematically while remaining grounded in core principles and responsive to rapid technological change.

The frames aren't separate from the gravitational model but rather:

- Shape how the system operates
- Guide movement between layers
- Explain system behavior
- Provide purpose and direction

When teaching AI literacy, this integration means:

- Recognizing the ethical implications (frame 1) of core forces. The model's ethical orientation, acting as a magnetic force, reinforces the frame of "AI development and use are ethical acts."
- Understanding how context (frame 2) shapes atmospheric patterns. The contextual atmosphere of multiliteracies supports the understanding that "AI systems are constructed and contextual."
- Considering the socio-technical implications (frame 3) of orbital elements. The interaction between core skills, multiliteracies, and AI competencies illustrates how "AI operates within socio-technical systems."
- Acknowledging evolution (frame 4) across all layers. The dynamic nature of orbiting AI competencies embodies the principle that "AI literacy is an evolving practice."
- Fostering collaboration (frame 5) throughout the system. The model's emphasis on the interplay between human skills and AI capabilities actualizes the frame of "AI is a collaborative co-intelligence."
- Empowering learners (frame 6) at each level. The model empowers librarians to guide patrons, reflecting the "AI literacy is empowering" frame.
- Encouraging reflection (frame 7) across all interactions. The continuous interaction and reconfiguration within the model encourage ongoing reflection, supporting "AI literacy deepens through reflective practice."

This integration creates a coherent system where frames provide the principles by which the gravitational model operates, while the model provides the structure through which the frames are expressed. By visualizing AI literacy as a dynamic system with durable skills at its core, multiliteracies as its atmosphere, and AI competencies as orbiting constellations, we create a flexible and adaptable framework for instruction that aligns with the seven frames.

This gravitational model provides librarians with a versatile tool for designing and implementing AI literacy instruction. It allows for integrating new AI developments while maintaining a strong foundation in enduring skills and established literacies. By leveraging this model, librarians can:

- Develop curricula that balance foundational skills with cutting-edge AI competencies

- Create instructional materials that illustrate the interconnected nature of various literacies and AI skills
- Design activities that encourage learners to reflect on their AI interactions and understand the ethical implications
- Adapt their instructional approaches as new AI technologies emerge without losing sight of core principles

Moreover, the model's flexibility allows it to be applied across different library types, from public libraries focusing on community AI literacy to academic libraries supporting advanced AI research. It provides a common language and conceptual framework for the library community to discuss and collaborate on AI literacy initiatives.

AI LITERACY: ESSENTIAL TO LIBRARIES IN THE AGE OF INTELLIGENCE

As described in chapter 2, libraries exist "in, of, and for the world" as stewards of (in)formation and transformation. The seven frames provide an ethical compass for AI adoption, offering a nuanced approach to understanding technological integration. As noted earlier, we believe that no catalyst has emerged with greater potential to unite libraries across ecosystems than AI literacy. We believe that providing AI literacy will be central to the work of libraries in the Age of Intelligence. For librarians, literacy instruction requires technical proficiency and an imaginative recognition of how AI tools can serve our core mission of connecting people with knowledge. Integrating AI literacy into library practice represents a continuation of our enduring mission and an evolution of our role in society.

Through our gravitational model of AI literacy—anchored by durable skills, enriched by multiple literacies, and responsive to emerging competencies—libraries can provide a stable framework for understanding and engaging with artificial intelligence. By grounding AI literacy in metaliteracy's integrated approach to learning, libraries can better prepare their communities for thoughtful AI engagement. The interaction between cognitive understanding, metacognitive reflection, behavioral adaptation, and affective awareness enables deeper learning and more effective navigation of AI's challenges and opportunities. AI literacy—which includes making informed, contextually aware decisions about technological tools—is crucial for librarians and learners alike. To this we turn in chapter 8 as we unpack our STACKS approach to leveraging generative AI.

NOTES

1. See Association of College and Research Libraries, "Framework for Information Literacy for Higher Education," 2016, www.ala.org/acrl/standards/ilframe work. At the time of this writing, the AI Competencies for Academic Library Workers that will be published by ACRL is in its initial comment period. The final form of those materials should release at the ALA Annual Conference in 2025 (the same time this book becomes available). This means that while we wish we could engage this here, we are forced to simply encourage you to see the results of their good work for yourselves.
2. See Trudi Jacobson and Tom Mackey, "2025 Metaliteracy Goals and Learning Objectives," *Metaliteracy*, 2025, https://metaliteracy.org/learning-objectives/metaliteracy-goals-and-learning-objectives-updated-2025/.
3. Several thoughtful frameworks for AI literacy have emerged recently, including Sandy Hervieux and Amanda Wheatley's "Building an AI Literacy Framework: Perspectives from Instruction Librarians and Current Information Literacy Tools," Choice White Paper (2024), which proposes a six-tier hierarchical approach to AI-literacy education. Other notable contributions include work by Kelly Mills et al., "AI Literacy: A Framework to Understand, Evaluate, and Use Emerging Technology," Digital Promise (2024), Hibbert et al., "A Framework for AI Literacy," *EDUCAUSE Review* (2024): 34–35, and Kong et al., "Evaluation of an Artificial Intelligence Literacy Course for University Students with Diverse Study Backgrounds," *Computers and Education: Artificial Intelligence* (2021). While our approach differs in its emphasis on metaliteracy and gravitational influence, these valuable contributions inform the evolving conversation about AI literacy in libraries.
4. A helpful paper exploring the four domains of metaliteracy and particularly how they relate to the ACRL Framework for Information Literacy for Higher Education can be found here: Diane Fulkerson et al., "Revisiting Metacognition and Metaliteracy in the ACRL Framework," *Communications in Information Literacy* 11, no. 1 (2017): 21, https://doi.org/10.15760/comminfolit.2017.11.1.45.

8

STACKS

An Approach for Learning, Problem-Solving, and Innovation with Generative AI

As artificial intelligence transforms how we discover, analyze, and create knowledge, libraries face an unprecedented opportunity to shape its integration across diverse communities and institutions. No catalyst has emerged with greater potential to unite libraries across ecosystems than AI literacy. It represents a natural evolution of our traditional mission and an acceleration of our core work, connecting people with knowledge in meaningful, ethical ways.

There are two major questions that libraries and librarians will be at the center of responding to as AI continues to enhance, accelerate, and redesign how we learn, solve problems, and innovate. First and foremost is the question of *how* we will do this work. In what ways will we pursue or be driven by our learning? How will learning be designed, implemented, and embodied with these newfound capabilities that extend beyond what people can accomplish without this technology? What kinds of essential and complementary skills will be crucial to effectively leverage these ever-advancing capacities?

The second question revolves around *when* and *why* we use such technologies. This has always been a concern with technological progress, from Plato and Phaedrus's dialogue[1] about how writing might make one more ignorant, to modern concerns about how computers might impact writing or calculators might harm our basic mathematical understanding. We often act as if technology will inevitably diminish learning, knowledge, and wisdom.

These two questions are why we developed STACKS, an approach to learning, problem-solving, and innovation both individually and collectively that can help us better determine and execute our own work and think critically and meaningfully about the capabilities and applications of generative AI that we enable and recommend. This approach will enable us to pursue these goals in ways that are human-centered, align with our values, and empower our work and our institutions.

THE FUTURE OF INQUIRY: WHY WE NEED NEW FRAMEWORKS

Before introducing our STACKS framework for addressing these challenges, it's crucial to understand four primary implications of artificial intelligence that are reshaping how we think about learning and knowledge:

1. *The removal of arbitrary limitations*: Throughout history, human learning has been constrained by access to information, the time available for study, memory limitations, and cognitive processing capacity. AI tools are redrawing or removing many of these barriers. For instance, large language models can now process context windows of over one million tokens—equivalent to more than 2,500 pages of text—far exceeding humans' working memory capacity.
2. *Unprecedented interconnectivity*: As human knowledge expands, individual expertise becomes an ever-shrinking fraction of collective knowledge. AI enables connections across previously siloed disciplines, allowing for the innovative cross-pollination of ideas. For example, AI systems can now create knowledge graphs spanning multiple disciplines, leading to unexpected insights and innovations.
3. *Accelerated discovery and innovation*: AI's ability to process information and generate insights at exponential speeds is transforming fields ranging from drug discovery to climate science. What once took years of research can now sometimes be accomplished in days or even hours. Consider AlphaFold2, whose creators were awarded half the 2024 Nobel Prize in Chemistry. AlphaFold2 can predict a protein's structure in minutes, a process that previously could take scientists years using traditional methods.[2]
4. *Enhanced knowledge accessibility*: AI tools are democratizing our access to complex information and analysis, making sophisticated research techniques available to broader audiences while raising new questions about information literacy and ethical use.

These developments make it clear that libraries need robust frameworks for implementing AI tools while maintaining their commitment to human-centered service and ethical information practices.

STACKS FOR LEARNING, PROBLEM-SOLVING, AND INNOVATION

One of our favorite experiences in libraries is walking the stacks—those rows of books that represent the physical organization of knowledge and enable serendipitous discovery. Building on this tradition, we developed STACKS as a framework for thoughtful AI implementation.

The term "stacks" has long been core to library identity, conveying the physicality of library collections and our commitment to ensuring access to a breadth of resources. STACKS expands this concept into a comprehensive approach to AI-empowered learning and work (see figure 8.1). Let's unpack each of these a little further as they relate to individual use.

- *Strategy*: This is the foundation of our approach to learning and problem-solving. Like surveying an obstacle course before starting, or

S	Strategy	The big picture, the overarching goals, and the general trajectory of our inquiry, learning, problem-solving, or innovation
T	Tactics	The concrete, incremental advancement of our strategy. It is the enacting of the next step of our pursuit.
A	Assembly	The collection of what we have identified, discovered, or created in the actualizing of our strategy and tactics
C	Curation	The distilling, interconnecting, and optimizing of our pursuit
K	Knowledge	The result of our strategy, tactics, assembly, and curation
S	Solutions	The application of the knowledge we acquired through this process

FIGURE 8.1
STACKS Framework

consulting a map before a journey, strategy helps us see the big picture. When working with AI tools, strategic thinking prevents us from over-relying on the technology, while ensuring that we develop lasting skills. It helps balance immediate gains with long-term growth.
- *Tactics*: These are the concrete steps that advance our strategy. Tactics keep us agile and responsive, and focused on the next immediate action while remaining open to serendipitous discoveries. Think of strategy as our trajectory and tactics as our actual movement—each step informed by what we learn along the way.
- *Assembly*: This is the gathering phase where we collect information, insights, and unexpected connections. Here, we organize our findings while staying mindful of how our habits and processes either enable or hinder our meaningful engagement with the material.
- *Curation*: This is the thoughtful organization of our assembled materials. If assembly puts ingredients on the counter, curation creates the recipe. We distill our learning, connect insights, and optimize content to make it useful and actionable.
- *Knowledge*: This is the product of our previous steps. Through systematic exploration and organization, we transform loose information into meaningful understanding. While valuable, knowledge alone isn't our end goal, though.
- *Solutions*: This is the practical application of our knowledge. Solutions move us from understanding to action. Without this step, our work—however insightful—remains abstract rather than contributing to real-world change. True wisdom emerges when knowledge leads to meaningful action.

STACKS IN ACTION

In an academic library, for example, we might think about a student who comes to us for help on a research project for class. The student is unsure of where they are headed but has a clear understanding of the kind of result that is expected of them. See figure 8.2 for an example of STACKS in action in this scenario.

While our academic library example demonstrates one application of STACKS, the framework adapts naturally to diverse library settings. For example, we might see:

S	Strategy	Understanding the assignment, research question, and the necessary approaches, information, and workflows that will be necessary for success
T	Tactics	Helping the student to understand the purpose, progression, and process of pursuing their work
A	Assembly	Organizing the information, research, and source materials that have been identified in their work thus far
C	Curation	Distilling, interconnecting, and aligning that information to the requirements and expectations of their assignment
K	Knowledge	The content and understanding necessary to effectively create and deliver the required work
S	Solutions	The actual creation and completion of the assignment with integrity and quality

FIGURE 8.2
STACKS in a Research Scenario

- *Public libraries* leverage STACKS to support community advocacy projects, where:
    » Skill identification focuses on civic literacy and data interpretation
    » Process planning incorporates local information sources and community knowledge
    » Tool selection considers how AI can empower organizing and outreach
- *Special libraries* adapt STACKS for specialized research needs, such as:
    » Supporting product development teams with technical literacy and trend analysis
    » Integrating domain-specific AI tools with proprietary databases
    » Documenting AI use for intellectual property considerations
- *School libraries* tailor STACKS for age-appropriate learning:
    » Breaking down complex topics into manageable components for young learners

» Guiding the supervised exploration of kid-friendly AI tools
» Incorporating digital citizenship and ethical AI use into instruction

This synergistic approach, enabled by STACKS, allows libraries of all types to draw on a single framework while tailoring their specific approach to their various contexts. It ensures that libraries can maintain their distinct missions while leveraging the enhanced capabilities made available to them by generative AI tools and platforms.

STACKS AND GENERATIVE AI TOOL ASSESSMENT AND ADOPTION

The STACKS framework can also be applied to the work of identifying, assessing, and deploying generative AI tools and platforms.[3] But before we walk through this, it is important that we first revisit the five core values that we established in chapter 2. Just as these values orient our broader approach to AI integration, they provide specific metrics for assessing tools and use cases. Each value offers both quantitative and qualitative measures for evaluation.

Transparency. Transparency in AI tools extends beyond mere technical documentation. It encompasses how a tool communicates its capabilities, limitations, and methodologies to users. Key considerations include:

- Do these tools give us insights into how their results were generated (e.g., showing reasoning, citing source materials, or providing information about their grounding)?
- Do they give us the ability to share our work from these tools with others (e.g., sharing a thread or publishing the results of our work with a tool)?

Transparency is essential for its capacity to foster trust, and to enable and sustain meaningful engagement with the results of our use of generative AI tools and platforms.

Curiosity. Tools that embody curiosity encourage exploration and discovery rather than simply providing answers. They create opportunities for serendipitous learning and unexpected connections. Essential elements include:

- Capacity to generate novel insights
- Support for serendipitous discovery
- Features that encourage exploration
- Potential for unexpected connections

Effective tools might facilitate this through interactive interfaces that encourage users to explore different paths or discover unexpected relationships between concepts.

Rigor. Rigor in AI tools transcends traditional notions of accuracy to encompass reliability, validity, and scholarly merit. This value ensures that tools meet the kinds of academic and disciplinary standards of our fields while supporting thoughtful research practices. Essential elements include:

- Accuracy and reliability of results
- Quality of data sources and processing
- Validation mechanisms (e.g., citations)

Tools that demonstrate a positive contribution to rigor might access authoritative sources, provide clear citation trails, and enable users to verify results against original sources.

Inclusion. Inclusion extends beyond basic accessibility to consider how tools serve diverse users and needs. This value examines both technical accessibility and broader questions of equity and representation. Key considerations include:

- Accessibility features and compliance
- Equitable access considerations
- Support for diverse users and needs
- Cost and barrier assessment

Tools that excel in inclusion might offer multiple modes of interaction, accommodate various approaches and abilities, and ensure affordability or access for different user groups.

Play. While play might seem secondary to academic tools, it represents a crucial aspect of engagement and learning. Play encourages experimentation, creativity, and deeper exploration. Essential elements include:

- User engagement and interface design
- Support for experimentation
- Enjoyable interaction patterns
- Features that encourage creative exploration

Strong tools in this category create environments where users feel comfortable experimenting and discovering, thus making learning effective and engaging.

So when it is time to embark on a new work of learning, problem-solving, or innovation, figure 8.3 is an example of how STACKS might help us think about the generative AI tools that we leverage for that pursuit.

Given all this, STACKS can be an agile yet robust framework for engaging the work of learning, problem-solving, and innovation in ways that are generative and sustainable. This is essential as the Age of Intelligence opens up new, more complex, and more impactful opportunities for our inquiry.

	Element	Overview	Primary Questions
S	Strategy	The big picture, the overarching goals, and the general trajectory of our inquiry, learning, problem-solving, or innovation.	What kinds of tools might we need for this work (e.g., search, literature review, strategy and planning, data analysis, code generation, image creation, etc.)?
T	Tactics	The concrete, incremental advancement of our strategy. It is the enacting of the next step of our pursuit.	In what order should we use the tools that we have identified, and what is their relationship to those used before and after the step we are on right now?
A	Assembly	The collection of what we have identified, discovered, or created in the actualizing of our strategy and tactics.	What tools might help us to capture, organize, and initially engage once we have acquired the information and materials that we were pursuing?
C	Curation	The distilling, interconnecting, and optimizing of our pursuit.	What are the most essential insights, connections, questions, and lines of inquiry that should be identified and explored at this stage of our work?
K	Knowledge	The result of our strategy, tactics, assembly, and curation.	What are the results of our learning, problem-solving, or innovation, and how do we begin to communicate them in the most effective manner possible?
S	Solutions	The application of the knowledge we acquired through this process.	What does this information do in the world? In what modalities, entities, and locations does it exist? How is it disseminated and engaged?

FIGURE 8.3

STACKS and Generative AI Tool Evaluation, Selection, and Application

A WORD ABOUT GENERATIVE AI, STACKS, AND THE FUTURE OF INQUIRY

As artificial intelligence transforms how we discover, analyze, and create knowledge, we face both unprecedented opportunities and challenges. Until now, human learning and problem-solving have been constrained by four fundamental limitations:

- Access limitations in both reaching and understanding information
- Time constraints on reading, processing, and analyzing information
- Memory limitations affecting information retention and recall
- Scale limitations on how much information we can cognitively process at once

AI tools have the potential to transcend these traditional boundaries. As described earlier, large language models can now process context windows exceeding one million tokens—equivalent to thousands of pages of text. AI systems can analyze vast data sets across disciplines, making connections beyond human cognitive capacity. Tools can retrieve and synthesize information nearly instantaneously, dramatically reducing time constraints.

Yet this expanded capability brings new challenges: How do we maintain human agency while leveraging these powerful tools? How do we ensure thoughtful implementation rather than passive dependence? The STACKS framework directly addresses the limitations of human cognition and learning, and can serve as a structured approach to overcome them through AI integration:

- *Strategy* tackles access limitations by helping us plan how to use AI tools to expand our reach and understanding of information.
- *Tactics* helps overcome time limitations by allowing us to break work into manageable steps and leverage AI for efficiency.
- *Assembly* addresses retention limitations by providing a framework to gather and organize information systematically, using AI as external memory.
- *Curation* helps manage scale limitations by giving us methods to distill and connect information that would otherwise exceed human cognitive capacity.

> STACKS is about understanding the tasks before us, selecting the right tool for the right job, and "stacking" multiple tools to enhance workflows for the best outcomes.

- *Knowledge and Solutions* transform these expanded capabilities into practical outcomes.

STACKS provides a structure for implementing AI tools thoughtfully while developing our own capabilities alongside them.

LIBRARIANS IN THE STACKS WITH AI LITERACY

Libraries and librarians must claim their central role in AI literacy and implementation because we are uniquely qualified to do so. Our training in information organization, our commitment to ethical information use, and our understanding of diverse community needs position us perfectly for this challenge.

The role of libraries in the AI era extends beyond tool adoption to include:

- Developing comprehensive AI literacy programs
- Creating ethical frameworks for AI implementation
- Supporting responsible innovation
- Ensuring equitable access to AI tools
- Preserving human agency in technological progress

As we move forward, our success will depend not just on the tools we choose to implement, but on how thoughtfully we approach their integration into our services and communities. Of course, all of this begs the question we've attempted to address throughout this book: Why libraries?

Although it may seem overwhelming, all that we've argued and proposed assumes the importance of libraries to not only be willing to enhance and expand their public impact on our shared but also to seize the responsibility and opportunity to provide the moral, ethical, and intellectual scaffolding for us to navigate this emerging world. In the foreseeable future, some of the greatest bottlenecks to progress with generative AI will not be about the tools themselves, but about the questions that have traditionally concerned libraries and librarians.

Who will help people to understand the kinds of skills and practices that are necessary for media and information literacy when an ever-increasing share of the information that we consume is at the very least touched by generative AI? Who will help individuals and industries develop the kinds of knowledge management systems and practices necessary to fully leverage the expanding capabilities of these generative AI tools? Who will provide the ethical grounding for how we deal with suppressed information, a flood of misinformation, and a society at large that currently lacks the information and media literacy skills to sort through all of these new realities?

Libraries and librarians must claim the center in all of these ways because we are uniquely qualified to do so. We are qualified because of our training and expertise. We are qualified because of our shared values and commitments to access, equity, inclusion, and truth. We are qualified because the strength, resolve, and collective power of our professional organizations makes them prepared and capable of navigating the world as it is so rapidly shifting. So, as we conclude this chapter and approach the end of this book, we offer three prepositions that synthesize our approach.

DOWN, OUT, UP: THREE PERSPECTIVES ON AI INTEGRATION

Within our specific contexts, librarians and staff embody our gravitational model: We are skilled professionals (gravitational core) engaged in librarianship (atmospheric context) that now, potentially, will be empowered by synergies with artificial intelligence (dynamic competencies as orbital constellations). As we thoughtfully prepare for AI integration, we will consider three perspectives informed by our model that keep library professionals at the center. Wherever you are—at the reference desk, behind a computer, engaging with learners, or buried behind stacks of research—take a moment to *look down, out,* and *up*. Each of these perspectives corresponds to a layer of our model and provides concrete ways to evaluate and approach AI opportunities.

Looking *down* at our feet represents attending to our fundamental work and existing workflows—the stable ground of durable skills that form our gravitational core. It signifies groundedness and stability: library professionals who understand and consider their existing competencies and workflows before considering changes. This protective stance ensures that we build AI integration on solid foundations rather than destabilizing effective practices.

Looking *out* examines our immediate context and the distant horizon—the atmospheric layer where our specific library roles, institutional contexts, and broader professional landscape inform how we approach AI integration. This dual perspective helps us understand both immediate opportunities and longer-term implications. Furthermore, the dual meaning of "looking out" (both as awareness and potential apprehension) captures many librarians' mixed emotions about AI integration.

Looking *up* encourages us to imagine possibilities within the orbital layer of dynamic AI competencies. This aspirational perspective transforms us from mere "workers" performing routine tasks into "solvers" who partner with AI to address complex challenges in novel ways. "Looking up" is also a hopeful phrase; it encourages librarians to imagine new ways of working and solving problems, reminding us to look up even as we feel overwhelmed by all we see. The depth of possibilities above is a space for imagination at play, a space of new promise and potential.

Together, these perspectives can guide balanced AI integration. The stability of looking down gives us the confidence to look up, while looking out provides crucial context for both. This framework can help librarians move beyond simply adapting to technological change; instead, we will actively shape how AI can enhance our professional practices. When library professionals across our ecosystem engage these three perspectives—grounded in our durable skills, aware of our contexts, and imaginative about possibilities—we collectively strengthen libraries' role as centers of gravity in an AI-literate society. Our steadfast attention to fundamental values and our willingness to imagine and shape new futures create the gravitational force that draws communities toward thoughtful, ethical, and empowering engagement with artificial intelligence. In this way, we don't just observe the horizon of technological change; we actively chart the course toward futures where libraries remain central, essential institutions in the service of human and ecological flourishing.

NOTES

1. Plato, *Euthyphro, Apology, Crito, Phaedo, Phaedrus*, vol. 1, Loeb Classical Library (Cambridge, MA: Harvard University Press, 1966), 275, http://data.perseus.org/citations/urn:cts:greekLit:tlg0059.tlg012.perseus-eng1:275.

2. Demis Hassabis, "AlphaFold Reveals the Structure of the Protein Universe," *Google DeepMind* (blog), July 28, 2022, https://deepmind.google/discover/blog/alphafold-reveals-the-structure-of-the-protein-universe/.

3. While STACKS embodies metaliteracy's multi-dimensional learning approach by intentionally engaging different learning domains, this chapter focuses on its immediate application to tool assessment and adoption. A comprehensive exploration of how STACKS empowers metaliteracy will be developed in forthcoming work. Here, we concentrate on providing practical frameworks for evaluating and integrating AI tools in library contexts.

Conclusion
First Steps for Libraries in the Age of Intelligence

In this book, we have tried to provide *initial* guidance and frameworks to make sense of some of the ways that generative AI presents us with real challenges, questions, and opportunities in a world that is good for the whole human family. In the book's first part, we tried to glimpse what this means for the future of learning and work, and explicitly what it means to do this work in a way that is unapologetically human-centered. We also provided some introductory grammar to make sense of key terms, ideas, and trajectories as they relate to generative AI so we can better connect, collaborate, and create together.

In the second part, we laid out an approach to thinking about AI integration and adoption, recognizing that these realities are filled with technical, ethical, social, economic, and institutional land mines and opportunities. We sought to provide some background and insight that can continue to shape both imagination and emerging implementation.

Finally, in the third part, we tried to be as concrete as we can in a world that is changing with ever-increasing speed. We have tried to show how our profession's deep roots, expertise, and instincts, captured in the practice of librarianship and documented in works like the ACRL Framework, give us a robust foundation on which to build. In our proposal of STACKS, we have offered a framework for navigating both our individual work and the assessment of generative AI tools as they continue to emerge.

We don't believe that all of this work can or should be the final word, the all-sufficient solution to all of our problems. Instead, we hope that this work has been an opportunity to prepare, to step out, and to begin. It is difficult to articulate both how early we are in the development and impact of generative AI and how far we have already come. The good news is that libraries are uniquely qualified for the work that this moment calls us to.

STEPS LIBRARIES CAN TAKE IN THE AGE OF INTELLIGENCE

Here, as we draw our proposals to a close, we wish to impart three last pieces of advice, not as experts, but as fellow travelers.

Our success in navigating the future is far more likely if we do it together. There are so many things pulling us in different and sometimes even opposing directions. There should always be space for complex, difficult, and important conversations about generative AI, but in order for us to claim the center in helping build a world for the whole human family, our commitment to navigating these conversations together must be unwavering and non-negotiable.

There are far more questions than answers right now, and this is why we must actively and assertively participate in the debate. Historically, changes in technology and their impact on our shared life have moved at a pace where we could more easily navigate the kinds of disruption that they've created. This will not be true with generative artificial intelligence and its impact on our shared life. It is precisely for this reason that we cannot retreat to our enclaves; we must not refuse to participate in rooms and communities where these questions are being raised (especially if they are not being addressed); and we must guide how others approach these questions even when their details are beyond our particular expertise. The work of librarianship and the ecosystem we have built can have a profoundly humanizing and transformative impact on how we build the future in real time.

We should not try to plan the entire journey but simply the next step (or two). As things continue to move so fast, we might be tempted to try and relieve some of the uncertainty and stress by attempting to predetermine how things will unfold. The reality is that this is simply not possible. We don't know how all of this will work out. We don't know the full scale, scope, and speed of the changes, opportunities, challenges, and risks that we will face. And for this reason, we must bring with us all of the resources, wisdom, experience, and ethics that we have to bear on our *next steps*.

FINAL WORDS

Throughout this book, we've explored how libraries serve as centers of gravity in an AI-enhanced world—stabilizing through ethical frameworks, connecting through collaboration, and energizing through innovation. Our gravitational model of AI literacy, seven frames, and STACKS framework provide practical tools for claiming this central role. As we navigate AI integration "in, of, and for" our communities, our libraries' traditional strengths—from information organization to ethical stewardship—become even more crucial.

As we conclude this exploration, we return to the fundamental concept of agency that has been threaded throughout our discussion. The future of libraries in the Age of Intelligence will be determined not by external forces but by how we choose to exercise our gravitational agency across personal, institutional, and ecosystem levels.

At the personal level, every librarian has the power to shape AI integration through daily choices and interactions. When you thoughtfully integrate AI tools into your workflows, guide patrons toward ethical AI use, or model critical engagement with these technologies, you exercise agency that ripples outward. These seemingly small but cumulatively powerful individual actions create the foundation for libraries' broader influence. Even in constrained circumstances with limited resources, each instance of personal agency contributes to the collective gravitational field of our profession.

At the institutional level, libraries have the power to establish themselves as essential guides in AI adoption and literacy. By creating AI ethics committees, developing instructional programs, forming strategic partnerships, and convening diverse stakeholders, your library can exercise institutional agency that transforms how your community engages with these technologies. When you position your library as an innovation hub or AI literacy center, you claim your rightful place at the center of this technological transformation.

At the ecosystem level, libraries have the collective power to shape policy, public discourse, and technological development and deployment. By actively reengaging and then participating in professional organizations, contributing to shared frameworks and standards, and speaking with a unified voice on crucial issues of AI ethics and implementation, you amplify libraries' gravitational influence beyond what any single institution could achieve. This ecosystem agency enables libraries across contexts to guide AI development toward human-centered outcomes that serve the public good.

Integrating these three spheres of agency creates a powerful gravitational force to guide AI development toward human flourishing while not only preserving but elevating libraries' essential role in society. But this force doesn't manifest automatically; it emerges only through conscious choice and deliberate action. The gravitational influence described throughout this book exists only as potential energy until activated through your agency—your choice to claim the center rather than remain at the periphery.

We believe that the future of libraries is bright. We believe that the values, skills, and wisdom of librarians and libraries can be some of the most vital contributions to what will become the next iteration of human learning and work. We believe that for far too long libraries have been excluded, ignored, and neglected, particularly regarding how important and how effective their work in the world has always been. We believe that what happens to libraries in the near future is not held in the hands of those who are outside of us, who don't understand and who cannot appreciate the humanity, the ingenuity, and the capabilities of librarians and libraries. We believe that the future of libraries is ours to set.

This is undoubtedly a risky reality. It will require us to take up space, to make our presence felt, to push back in some places, and to provide a push of support in others. This may lie outside of our experience and even outside of our comfort zone, but because we believe in our work and in the mission of librarians and libraries, it is our *responsibility*.

Librarians and libraries *are* the gravitational centers of human learning, whether we get the credit for it or not. This is a once-in-a-lifetime opportunity for us to make that clear, not in a way that is arrogant or self-serving but that is explicitly and unapologetically for the sake of those we serve and beyond.

We must remember that as centers of gravity, we are both a stabilizing and an animating force. We are a stabilizing force because our work draws on a rich tradition and history of curating and enhancing human learning, enabling us to work for the construction of a more just, equitable, and generous world. But we are also an animating force, fierce in our advocacy of the forgotten, the left behind, and the underdog. We provide a foundation from which to build, and a clear-eyed vision not only of what is possible but what should be.

We believe that generative AI presents libraries and librarians with an unprecedented opportunity to shape and reshape the world into the kind of place that we have been quietly, carefully, intentionally, and creatively building all along—but now we can do so at a speed, scale, and scope that was formerly confined to the realm of fantasy or delusion.

Libraries are a gravitational force, "the strong one under the floor," the highly capable, thoughtful, and generative community of practice that is uniquely prepared for this moment. Some might take the opportunity at a moment like this to suggest that libraries need to "move beyond" the ways they have done things in the past, and that a new kind of library and librarianship must emerge. We believe that such an approach is absolutely wrong.

The library ecosystem, and the librarians who cultivate and sustain it, must instead recommit themselves to the core of their work: their skills, ethics, and values. These must become clearer, more explicit, and more unapologetic. They are the animating force behind everything we seek to do in and for the world. We must firmly plant ourselves on the ground on which we already stand, both literally as a tangible and physical presence in our communities, and metaphorically in our commitment and capacity to the kinds of literacies necessary to do our work and serve our constituents. Libraries must not take leave of the things that have always been part of our work.

What is next is not a kind of leaving behind. We are not looking out at the horizon trying to anticipate an entirely new place where we must travel. Instead, we assert that libraries and library workers, across the ecosystem, must commit themselves to looking *up*. Rooted and grounded in who we have always been, there is an ever-expanding space for us to shape, guide, and protect the future world we wish to build and to inhabit.

The only question that remains now is this: *Will we claim the center?*

About the Authors

Michael Hanegan is the founder and chief research officer of the Center for the Future of Learning and Work. He is an adjunct professor at Rose State College and the University of Central Oklahoma. His research and practice spans K–12 schools, higher education, the library ecosystem, and industry to cultivate and sustain human-centered approaches to the future of learning and work. He lives in Edmond, Oklahoma.

Chris Rosser is a first year and transfer experience librarian at Oklahoma State University. From 2009 to 2024, he served as an instructional and theological librarian at Oklahoma Christian University. His expertise centers on pedagogy, instructional design, and innovative approaches to learning, including gamification and AI-empowered learning. His work has been featured at ALA's annual conference and at several other conferences for libraries and scholars. He lives in Edmond, Oklahoma.

Index

A
academic libraries
    claiming the center, 9
    skills-based economy and, 11
    STACKS in action, 120-121
    transformation of ecosystem for AI, 30
access
    equity of access to AI, 85
    limitations on learning/problem-solving, 125
accessibility, 118, 123
ACRL Framework for Information Literacy for Higher Education, 95, 99, 100-102
action, 22, 27
Active Explorer, 69-70, 74-75
adaptability
    adaptive implementation, 9
    of AI Literacy Framework, 102, 103
    culture of, 83
    durable skills *vs.* dynamic AI competencies, 111
    skills and, 81, 107
adoption
    AI, 65-77
    definition of, 51
    libraries shifting from access to, 52-53
    meaning of, 65-66
advocacy, 82, 109
affective domain, 42, 44, 45, 95-96
Age of Intelligence
    AI literacy as essential in, 114-115
    between/below spatial planes in, 17-18
    enhanced library in, 13-14
    foundational principles for, ix-xi
    gravitational agency of libraries in, 7
    libraries as centers of gravity in, xvi, 3, 4
    libraries as foundational presence, vii, viii
    libraries claiming the center in, 8, 91, 130
    metaliteracy in, 95
agency
    collaborative co-intelligence and, 39
    with convening approach, 58, 59
    enhanced agency of libraries, 14
    at ethical horizon, 21-22
    gravitational agency, 6-7, 131-133
    human-centered, 18, 20, 30-31, 125-126
    innovation hubs for gravitational agency, 88-90
    in orienting questions, 27-29
AI
    See artificial intelligence
algorithmic systems, 38
AlphaFold2, 118
American Library Association (ALA), xvi, 7, 15
Amodei, Dario, xi
arrival technology, ix, 37, 57-58
artificial intelligence (AI)
    AI Literacy Framework, 96-97, 100-103
    adoption of, 65-77
    budget/resource allocation, 84-87
    claiming the center, principles of, xiv-xv
    collaborative co-intelligence, 39-40
    competencies of, 109-112
    concepts/definitions, 33-46

{ 137 }

138 | Index

artificial intelligence *(cont.)*
    conclusion about, 129-133
    core values for AI integration, 23-25
    costs and possibilities of AI integration, 79-91
    durable skills and, 97-99, 105-107
    evaluating implementation of, 29
    ethical horizon, 21-22
    failed approaches to learning/development, 67-68
    gravitational model, 103-105, 112-114
    human-centered paradigm, 19-21
    implications on learning/knowledge, 118-119
    Interest and Readiness Matrix, 68-71
    integration process, 51-64
    key technologies of, 35-38
    Learning Design Framework, 72-74
    Librarians'/libraries' role in AI literacy, 126-127
    libraries as innovation hubs, 87-90
    library ecosystem, transformation of, 29-31
    library positioning between/below and, 17-18
    metaliteracy and, 42-46, 95-96
    orienting questions, 26, 27-29
    perspectives on AI integration, 127-128
    questions for libraries/librarians about, 117-118
    seven frames of AI literacy, 99-100
    STACKS and,119-124
    UTAUT2 model, 66-67
    See also generative artificial intelligence (GenAI)
"Artificial Intelligence and the Future of Theological Education" (Hanegan & Rosser), viii
atmosphere
    dynamic AI competencies as orbital, 109-112
    of gravitational model, 104-105
    of multiliteracies, 113
automation, 12, 83-84

B
behavioral domain, 42, 44, 45, 95-96
budgets and budgetary allocation, 84-87

C
carbon emissions, x
center of gravity
    AI literacy education by libraries, 100
    claiming, in shifting information landscape, 7-10
    convening approach for AI integration and, 60
    gravitational agency, 6-7
    libraries as, 3-4, 5, 30-31
    libraries as vital centers of gravity, 17-18
    libraries' exercise of gravitational agency, 131-133
    library ecosystem transformation, 29-31
change, 83-84
ChatGPT, ix
Chosen Holdout, 69-70, 75
claiming the center
    Age of Intelligence and, 8, 91, 130
    key principles of, xiv-xv
    libraries as center of gravity, 3-4
    libraries claiming their place, 90-91
    shared grammar for AI, 15
    through service to community, xvi
cognitive domain
    AI literacy as metaliteracy in practice, 45
    of metaliteracy, 42, 43, 95-96
collaboration, 113
collaborative co-creation, 42, 44-45
collaborative co-intelligence
    AI is a collaborative co-intelligence frame, 100
    description of, 39
    as imagination in action, 39-40
    synergy with, 33
commitment to equity of outcome, 70
community
    engagement skills of librarians, 81
    input for AI Literacy Framework, 102
    multiliteracies as contextual ground of AI literacy, 109
competencies, dynamic AI
    actualizing AI literacy through gravitational model, 112-114
    characteristics of, 109-110
    durable skills and, 107
    durable skills *vs*., 111-112
    in gravitational model of AI literacy, 104, 105
    implications for librarians, 110
    as orbital atmosphere, 109-112
computational thinking, 98
connections
    AI tool assessment, 122-123
    from engagement with AI, 86-87
    libraries as connecting forces, 5
contextual ground, 107-109
convening approach, 58-60

Index | 139

core
  durable skills as gravitational core of AI literacy, 105–107
  dynamic AI competencies interaction with, 109
  of gravitational model, 103–105
  in Learning Design Framework, 74
core needs, 63
core values
  AI integration and, 23–25, 62
  AI tool assessment, 122–124
  AI's effects through lens of, 28
  discerning values in tools, 25–26
  innovation hubs grounded in, 89
critical evaluation, 107
cross-functional team, 61–62
curation
  by libraries in Age of Intelligence, 10
  navigating imagination in AI integration, 40–41
  in STACKS framework,, 119, 120, 121, 124, 125
curators
  behavioral domain, 45
  navigating imagination in AI, 33, 40–41
curiosity
  for AI adoption, 75
  AI tool assessment, 122–123
  AI's effects through lens of core values, 28
  as core value, 23–25
  interest as indicator of, 68
Curious Novice, 69–70, 75

D

data literacy, 97
decentralized learning, 11
Detached Participant, 69–70, 75–76
development, 67–68
digital literacy, 97
discovery
  accelerated discovery with AI, 118
  AI tool assessment, 122–123
  curiosity fosters spirit of, 23–24
documentation, 82
durable skills
  actualizing AI literacy through gravitational model, 112–114
  at core of AI literacy, 97
  dynamic AI competencies vs., 111–112
  as gravitational core of AI literacy, 105–107
  in gravitational model, 103, 104
dynamic AI competencies
  See competencies, dynamic AI

E

ecosystem agency, 6–7
ecosystem level
  convening approach at, 59
  innovation hubs at, 89
  libraries' exercise of gravitational agency, 131–132
  orienting questions at, 27
efficiency, 83, 85
electricity, ix
elements, of AI adoption, 71–72, 74–76
emotional intelligence, 44
empowerment, 100, 113
energizing forces, 5–6
enhanced library, 13–14
environmental concerns, 3
equity
  of access to AI, 85, 86
  AI adoption and, 52
  AI tools for inclusion, 123
  commitment to equity of outcome, 70
  innovation hubs and, 89
  libraries' values, xiv
ethical frameworks, x
ethical horizon
  AI synergies "for the world," 20
  description of, 21–22
  imagination for shaping, 22–23
  libraries as centers of gravity in AI landscape, 30–31
ethical literacy, 98
ethics
  actualizing AI literacy through gravitational model, 112–114
  AI development and use are ethical acts frame, 99
  AI literacy as orienting, ethical practice, 96–97
  algorithmic systems and, 38
  concerns about generative AI, ix–x
  dynamic AI competencies and, 110
  ethical horizon, 21–22
  GenAI and, 37
  in gravitational model of AI literacy, 103, 104
  imagination for shaping, 22–23
  large language models and, 35–36
  librarians/libraries central role in AI literacy, 126–127
  libraries as stabilizing institutions, 4
  "in, of, and for the world" framework, 19–21

evolution
    of AI literacy, 113
    of contextual ground, 108
existential implications, of AI, 19
experimentation, 85, 123
expertise, 8

F
fear, 34
"For the World" dimension, 20
frameworks
    ACRL Framework for Information Literacy for Higher Education, 95, 99, 100-102
    four-fold framework for AI integration, 53-55
    for libraries as centers of gravity, xiii-xiv
    organization of book, xv-xvi
    STACKS, 117-128
future of learning/work in libraries
    AI integration and, 54
    claiming center in shifting information landscape, 7-10
    enhanced library, 13-14
    gravitational agency, exerting influence across library ecosystem, 6-7
    larger trends/trajectories, 10-13
    libraries as center of gravity and stabilizing forces, 3-6, 131-133
    shared grammar for AI, 14-15
    success in navigating together, 130

G
generative artificial intelligence (GenAI)
    Age of Intelligence and, ix-xi, 13-14
    author's use of, xi-xiii
    author's work with, viii
    benefits/risks of, xi
    budget/resource allocation for, 84-87
    claiming center in shifting information landscape, 7-10
    collaborative co-intelligence, 39-40
    conclusion about, 129-133
    frameworks for libraries as centers of gravity, xiii-xiv
    gravitational agency, 6-7
    implications on learning/knowledge, 118-119
    larger trends/trajectories and, 10-13
    librarians'/libraries' role in AI literacy, 126-127
    libraries as center of gravity and stabilizing forces, 3-6

libraries' role in technological change, vii-viii
    metaliteracy in use of, 44-45
    STACKS, generative AI tool assessment/adoption, 122-124
    technical description of, 36-37
geographic location, 82
goals, 62-63
grammar
    for AI adoption, 71-72, 74, 75
    shared grammar for AI, 14-15
    use of AI tools for, xii
gravitational agency
    convening approach as, 58-60
    exerting influence across library ecosystem, 6-7
    innovation hubs for, 88-90
    libraries as gravitational force, 133
    libraries' exercise of, 131-133
    in orienting questions, 26, 27-29
gravitational influence
    larger trends/trajectories and, 10-11
    library positioning between/below and, 18
gravitational model, 103-105, 107-115, 127-128
gravity
    See center of gravity
ground
    dynamic AI competencies interaction with, 109
    of gravitational model, 104-105
    multiliteracies as contextual ground, 107-109

H
habit, 72, 75
Hanegan, Michael, viii, xi-xiii, 135
holistic approach, 102
human being
    agency, 18, 125-126
    AI integration, human-centered, 53-54, 82
    human side of technological change, 83-84
    human-AI collaboration, 39-40
    orienting questions for evaluating AI's impact, 26, 27-29
human-centered paradigm
    AI implementation, evaluation of, 29
    conclusion about, 31-32
    core values for AI integration, 23-25
    ethical horizon, 21-22
    in framework for AI integration, 53-54
    imagination for shaping ethical horizon, 22-23

libraries as centers of gravity, 17-18
orienting questions for, 26, 27-29
overview of, 19-21
responsibility to exercise agency, 30-31
transforming library ecosystem, 29-31
values in tools, discerning, 25-26

I

imagination
about AI, 34-35
AI integration and, 40-41, 46
collaborative co-intelligence, 39-40
gravitational pull and, 46
importance of, 34-35
of librarians/libraries, unleashing, 90-91
metaliteracy for expanding, 41-45
for shaping ethical horizon, 22-23
implementation
adoption, gap between, 76-77
adoption vs., 65-66
definition of, 51
improvisation, 25, 26
"in, of, and for the world" framework, 19-21
inclusion
AI adoption and, 52
AI tool assessment, 123
as core value for AI integration, 24, 25, 28-29
discerning values in tools, 26
individual particularity, 71
influence, 9, 18
information architecture, 80
information discovery, 107
information literacy, 41-42, 97
(in)formational stability, 4
infrastructure, 81-82
innovation hubs, 87-90
institutional level
convening approach at, 59
innovation hubs at, 88
libraries' exercise of gravitational agency, 131
orienting questions at, 27
instructional focus, 111
integration
AI integration process, 51-64
definition of, 52
librarians as cultivators of durable skills, 107
intelligence
See artificial intelligence; collaborative co-intelligence

interconnectivity, 101, 118
interest, as approach to learning, 68-71
Interest and Readiness Matrix, 69-71, 74-76

J

Jacobson, Thomas, 41
"jagged frontier" metaphor, 55
Japanese philosophy, vii, xiv, xvi, 17, 133
jobs
See work

K

knowledge
GenAI and, 9-10
implications of AI on, 118-119
skills of librarians, 80, 81
in STACKS framework, 119, 120, 121, 124, 126

L

large language models (LLMs), 35-36
learning
culture of continuous, 83
decentralized learning, 11
failed approaches to, 67-68
human-centered paradigm for AI integration, 19-21
implications of AI on learning/knowledge, 118-119
Interest and Readiness Matrix for, 68-71
multiliteracies/durable skills, 97-99
play creates space for, 24-25
STACKS and, 119-120, 122-126
Learning Design Framework, 72-76
librarians
AI adoption, importance of, 76-77
AI integration, perspectives on, 127-128
AI integration and, 55-58, 60-63
AI literacy instruction guided by, 98-99
convening approach for AI integration, 58-60
culture of continuous learning, 83
as durable skills cultivators, 106-107
gravitational agency of, 6
human side of technological change, 83-84
imagination of, 90-91
infrastructure/process for AI integration, 81-82
innovation hubs for gravitational agency, 88-90
multiliteracies as contextual ground of AI literacy, 108-109

Index | 141

librarians *(cont.)*
    orienting questions for evaluating AI's impact, 26, 27–29
    as priests, prophets, curators, 40–41
    questions about AI for, 117–118
    role in AI literacy, 126–127
    steps to take in Age of Intelligence, 130
    "work behind the work" for AI integration, 79–81
libraries
    access to adoption shift, 52–53
    AI adoption, importance of, 76–77
    AI integration and, 21, 53–63, 79–82
    AI literacy and, 96, 114–115
    AI technologies for, 35–38
    budget/resource allocation for AI initiatives, 84–87
    as centers of gravity and stabilizing forces, xiii–xiv, 3–6, 17–18, 131–133
    claiming center, xiv–xv, 4, 7–10, 15, 90–91, 130
    culture of continuous learning, 83
    dynamic AI competencies and, 110
    at ethical horizon, 21–23
    generative AI, role in transformation, vii–viii
    as hubs for AI innovation, 87–88
    human-centered paradigm for AI integration, 19–21
    imagination of, 90–91
    innovation hubs for gravitational agency, 88–90
    larger trends/trajectories, 10–13
    questions about AI for, 117–118
    role in AI literacy, 126–127
    shared grammar for AI, 14–15
    STACKS in action, 120–122
    steps to take in Age of Intelligence, 130
library ecosystem, 27, 29–31, 39–40, 59, 100
limitations, 118, 125–126
literacy, 60, 70
    See also artificial intelligence (AI) literacy; metaliteracy, multiliteracies
LLMs (large language models), 35–36

M

machine learning, 36
Mackey, Trudi, 41
media literacy, 97
mediating role, 108
memory limitations, 125
metacognition, 101

metacognitive domain, 42, 43, 45, 95–96
metaliteracy
    ACRL Framework for Information Literacy, alignment with, 100–102
    AI literacy and, 34, 45–46, 95–115
    AI Literacy Framework, evolving nature of, 102–103
    dynamic AI competencies and, 109–112
    four domains of, 43–45
    in framework for AI integration, 54
    multiliteracies and, 97–99, 107–109
    overview of, 41–42, 95–96
Metaliteracy Goals and Learning Objectives, 98
motivation, 72, 75–76
multiliteracies
    AI literacy intersection with, 97–99
    as contextual ground of AI literacy, 107–109
    in gravitational model, 104, 112–114
    seven frames of AI literacy, 99–100

N

natural language processing, 36
needs, core, 63
neural networks, 36, 37

O

opportunities, 86–87
orbital atmosphere, 109–112
orienting questions, 26, 27–29

P

personal level
    AI integration at, 131
    convening approach at, 58
    innovation hubs at, 88
    orienting questions at, 27
perspectives, on AI integration, 127–128
planning
    for AI integration, 63–64
    dynamic AI competencies and, 110
    for next steps, 130
play
    AI tool assessment, 123
    as core value for AI integration, 24–25
    discerning values in tools, 26
practical implementation, 19
principles, core, xiii–xiv
problem-solving, using STACKS, 119–120, 122–124, 125–126
process management, 81
professional organizations, 15
prophets and priests, xvi, 14–15, 40–41

protopia, 22-23
public libraries
    skills-based economy and, 11
    STACKS in, 121
    transformation of ecosystem for AI, 30

Q

questions
    about AI, 53-54, 62-63, 87, 117-118, 130
    behind the questions, 80
    orienting questions, 26, 27-29

R

readiness, as approach to learning, 68-71
reflection
    actualizing AI literacy through gravitational model, 113
    reflective adaptation, 102
    reflective practice for AI literacy, 100, 101
research
    accelerated discovery with AI, 118
    AI for assisting students with research, 86-87
    STACKS in actions, 120-122
resource allocation, 84-87, 110
"right tool, right job," 55
rigor
    AI tool assessment, 123
    as core value, 24, 25, 28
    discerning values in tools, 26
risks, xi
road map, for AI integration, 60-63
Rosser, Chris, viii, xi-xiii, 135

S

school libraries
    gravitational influence of, 30
    skills-based economy and, 11
    STACKS, use of, 121-122
Scientific Reports, x
sequential approach, 57
service design, 108
seven frames of AI literacy, 100-102, 112-114
shaping force, 106
skills
    AI adoption and, 72, 75-76
    for AI integration, 79-82
    development of, 11
    durable skills, 97-99, 103, 104, 105-107
    dynamic AI competencies, 110, 111-112
    readiness as indicator of, 68
    skill transfer facilitator, 108

    skills-based economy, 11
    up-skilling/re-skilling, 12
special libraries, 30, 121
stability
    below intersection for, 18
    durable skills *vs.* dynamic AI competencies, 111
    gravitational properties of durable skills, 106
    libraries as center, 3, 4, 6, 9
STACKS framework
    in action, 120-122
    AI integration, perspectives on, 127-128
    generative AI tool assessment and, 122-124
    implications of AI on learning/knowledge, 118-119
    librarians' role in AI literacy, 126-127
    overview of, 119-120
    questions about AI, 117-118
    as structure for implementing AI tools, 125-126
stakeholders
    approach for AI integration and, 55-58, 60
    institutional agency and, 7
    libraries as connecting forces, 5
"strong one under the floor" metaphor, vii, xiv, xvi, 17, 90, 133
students, 86-87

T

targeted content progression, 71
technology
    adoption of AI, 65-77
    AI Literacy Framework, responsiveness of, 102
    ethical concerns about generative AI, ix-x
    technological change, 83-84
    larger trends/trajectories, 10-13
    libraries' role and, vii-viii, 7-8
    questions for libraries/librarians about AI, 117-118
terminology
    of AI integration, 51-52
    grammar as AI adoption element, 71-72
    shared grammar for AI, 14-15
"third places," 9
transferability, 106
translation, 26
transparency
    AI tool assessment, 122
    AI's effects through lens of core values, 28
    core value, 23, 25

U

universal applicability, 106
up-skilling, 12
UTAUT2 (unified theory of acceptance and use of technology 2) model, 66-67

V

values
    AI integration and, 62
    convening approach grounded in, 59
    core values and, 23-25, 28, 122-124
    gravitational model and, 103, 104, 112-114
    of libraries/librarians, xiv, 4, 14, 132
    in tools, discerning, 25-26
visual literacy, 98
vocabulary
    See terminology
voluntary, opt-in approach, 57-58

W

work
    AI for job search, 86
    AI for mundane/repetitive tasks, 87
    technological change and, 83-84
    human-centered paradigm for AI integration, 19-21

www.ingramcontent.com/pod-product-compliance
Lightning Source LLC
Chambersburg PA
CBHW052028141125
35353CB00055B/591